D1316184

PRAISE FOR *THEY SAID THEY WANTED REVOLUTION*

"Illuminating, poignant. An inspiring read."

—Azar Nafisi, author of *Reading Lolita in Tehran*

"A wonder of reporting and reflection. Neda Toloui-Semnani's masterly, propulsive historical narrative leads the reader to an uncannily sharp view on the present. This is an essential book in the canon of stories that pursue a universal question: How can our parents know us so intimately and remain out of reach at the same time?"

—Stephanie Gorton, author of *Citizen Reporters*

"Neda Toloui-Semnani gifts us a unique memoir—heartbreaking, poetic, and ultimately inspiring—of revolution and its effects, ones that haunt its children for decades. The old quote (turned old cliché) that a revolution devours its own (or its children) is not just a truism for Neda's Persian family but a tragedy that came to define her. This history—of not just revolution but also dual identity—is seldom told with such raw emotion and devastating beauty."

—Hooman Majd, author of *The Ayatollah Begs to Differ*

"*They Said They Wanted Revolution* by Neda Toloui-Semnani belongs to a growing body of memoirs, like *The Return* by Hisham Matar and *The Window Seat* by Aminatta Forna, that illuminate the global world in which we all now live, with its violently crisscrossing perspectives. Toloui-Semnani's parents, young Iranian Americans, were inspired by the Berkeley Free Speech Movement to promote revolution in Iran—and got Khomeini's hell. When her father is executed, her pregnant mother flees with three-year-old Neda across the desert on horseback—back to California. The new way that the author sees the United States after her dive into this riveting story is a gift. Her complex, tragic understanding of political passion is gold."

—Suzannah Lessard, author of *The Absent Hand*

"Neda Toloui-Semnani delivers a deeply intimate look at the most critical years in contemporary Iranian history—the revolution—with a portrait of her family that will offer so many readers insights into Iran's dilemmas today. The multigenerational experience of our culture often lives only in data and newsprint, almost always hinging on politics and theory, but Toloui-Semnani lets us join her in exploring personal, emotional, and even spiritual dimensions. The result is a book that is as hard to put down as it is to part with. In untangling the layers of her own personal history, Toloui-Semnani so generously writes us all into her powerful and beautiful debut."

—Porochista Khakpour, author of the acclaimed
Brown Album: Essays on Exile and Identity

"A richly informative book that simultaneously informs, moves, inspires, and gracefully captures a difficult time in Iranian history with honesty and candor. Neda Toloui-Semnani's intimate memoir artfully intertwines her parents' coming-of-age against the backdrop of pre-revolutionary Tehran with her own journey of self-discovery as the child of two passionate, risk-taking political activists. From California to Iran to Turkey, this gripping, beautiful account of a woman's reckoning with her parents' history, of the treacherous path of being smuggled out of Iran, paints a vivid and haunting picture of the lives of those fighting for justice. An important, riveting page-turner filled with luminous prose."

—Natasha Scripture, author of *Man Fast: A Memoir*

"Exhilarating and contemplative in turns, Neda Toloui-Semnani's family memoir is both history and her story. Part bildungsroman and part investigative journalism, she sets out on a journey to discover her past, looking for clues in places as diverse as Missouri and Berkeley, Yemen and Baghdad. She tells us not only about the entangled modern histories of Iran and the United States but also of the shifting meanings of morality and love, rebellion and justice. An outstanding read."

—Arash Azizi, author of *The Shadow Commander: Soleimani, the US, and Iran's Global Ambitions*

"Neda Toloui-Semnani has given us the most generous book. Like the hyphen in her storied family name, she sits in the liminal, holding two worlds, two nations, two generations together, and suturing with such a deft touch many sides of twin wounds: the loss of her progressive Iranian parents. Toloui-Semnani's commitment to truth, art, and family is exemplary, showing us all what creative nonfiction can be: journalism as literature, family lore as history, and history as inheritance. This book goes beyond telling a story. It reclaims it, giving back to a brave, intelligent, and dutiful daughter all that she set out to find: revolutionary love that holds together tomorrow, today, and the ever-elusive details of yesterday. *They Said They Wanted Revolution* made me fall in love with the craft all over again."

—Cinelle Barnes, author of *Monsoon Mansion* and *Malaya*

"A daughter's profoundly moving and meticulous quest to understand her father's execution and her family's expulsion from home, this book is brimming with lyrical beauty and cerebral brilliance. In precise, journalistic prose that erupts in a dazzling emotional crescendo, Toloui-Semnani captures the shape of loss and arc of resilience. An extraordinary meditation on love, loss, and the cost of redirecting history, *They Said They Wanted Revolution* is a vital story for our times."

—Jean Guerrero, author of *Hatemonger: Stephen Miller, Donald Trump, and the White Nationalist Agenda* and *Crux: A Cross-Border Memoir*

THEY

SAID

THEY

WANTED

REVOLUTION

THEY
SAID
THEY
WANTED
REVOLUTION

A MEMOIR OF
MY PARENTS

NEDA TOLOUI-SEMNANI

Published by Little A, New York

www.apub.com

Amazon, the Amazon logo, and Little A are trademarks of Amazon.com, Inc., or its
affiliates.

"Bookends"
Words and Music by Paul Simon
© Songs of Universal, Inc. on behalf of Paul Simon Music (BMI)
Used by Permission - All Rights Reserved

ISBN-13: 9781542004480 (hardcover)
ISBN-10: 1542004489 (hardcover)

ISBN-13: 9781542004497 (paperback)
ISBN-10: 1542004497 (paperback)

Cover illustration by Mina M. Jafari

Cover design by Faceout Studio, Spencer Fuller

Interior photo courtesy of the author

Printed in the United States of America

First edition

To my parents

For my Rumi

AUTHOR'S NOTE

This is a reported memoir. A piece of nonfiction, yes, but it is my own interpretation of facts and events. All names of those living have been changed except for those of my brother and me. Some dialogue and scenes were reconstructed based on extensive interviews and years of research. Italics indicate dialogue that is reconstructed or imagined. Double quotation marks (" ") indicate quotes that I witnessed, recorded, or have been able to confirm.

PROLOGUE

It was Friday at the end of May. The dying days of spring, 2020. I was driving into Manhattan from my home in Brooklyn. It wasn't just the first time in four months that I was entering the city. It was also the first time I had chosen to leave my apartment to go farther than the nearby park or the grocery store half a block away.

New York City, or at least my small corner of it, was still largely quiet then, except for the ambulance sirens. The passing days were marked by that sound and by other musical interludes: the bars of "Pop Goes the Weasel" broadcast from the speakers of a dedicated ice cream truck; the improvised jazz played by a saxophonist somewhere in the cluster of nearby buildings, and, every night at 7:00 p.m., the percussive applause celebrating the health-care workers and first responders trying to save us from a new virus.

But the city's usual noises—honking traffic, children playing, trucks idling, and neighbors shouting, the general din of city life—had been snuffed out. Once night fell, it was still and quiet, except for the sirens. We were in the third month of lockdown, and many who had remained in New York City, which was then the epicenter of this new pandemic, hadn't survived April. Those of us who had made it through were grieving and worried about what the summer would hold.

And now, something else was beginning. Earlier that week, on Memorial Day, George Floyd—a Black man—had been killed by police in Minneapolis, Minnesota. Protests against police brutality and for racial justice had started there but were beginning to spread to other cities and states. The new civil rights movement, one that had started years earlier with the killings of Trayvon Martin and Michael Brown, was reigniting.

The night before, scrolling through social media postings, I'd seen footage of a protest held in Union Square. I watched officers from the New York City Police Department pull people from the demonstration and into the police vans. The images brought me up short: In this city we had just watched makeshift hospitals built and refrigerated trailer trucks turned into morgues. We knew the threat of the virus and how to keep ourselves safe: distance, hygiene, and masks.

And yet, here were protesters pushed together. Their masked faces, their loud cries, and their wide eyes revealing both grief and rage. Rage, which is more than anger. Rage, which needs release and so demands action. Rage, which grows and grows and grows like fire.

It was clear to me that something was breaking open. I was sure of this, the way a journalist sometimes just knows a story is about to begin but can't explain how they know.

The next day, with my reporter's notebook in hand, I arrived at Union Square and walked to the steps overlooking 14th Street. I introduced myself to a handful of people, all masked, who were finishing up writing on their cardboard signs. There were bouquets at their feet. They told me the flowers were for a vigil for Floyd, scheduled to take place in downtown Brooklyn later in the afternoon. But first they were heading down to City Hall, where people were gathering.

I looked up and nodded toward the scrum of roughly fifty NYPD officers and the dozen police vans.

"Are you nervous?" I asked one of the young men, a student in his early twenties.

He shook his head. He told me that as a Black Latino, he felt his place was to be on the streets demanding justice, even if that meant risking his arrest, his safety, and his health.

I glanced at the cops and the vans and then back at the young, thin man with his mask pulled down under his chin, revealing a broad, infectious smile. My heart tightened for a moment. In his face was the echoed image of so many before him—students who'd marched face to face with injustice and had demanded the status quo bend to their will.

I saw in his face a glancing shadow of other twentysomethings who'd marched, planned, and plotted until eventually the world gave way: power structures toppled, new structures rose up from the ruins. That is to say, I saw my parents as they were when they were young, reflected in the face of this stranger.

Over the course of the next few weeks, the city roared to life: largely peaceful protests were met with tear gas, pepper spray, and circling police helicopters. Police drove their cars into crowds, officers trapped and beat demonstrators, and journalists were regularly arrested. I helped cover these stories for VICE News, in print and on television. I climbed a lamp pole to get a better view of confrontations, spoke to cops and bystanders, and bent low to the street in order to weave my way between bodies so I could watch riot cops begin their sweeps.

Each day of unrest reminded me of the stories I'd heard, studied, and collected about my parents, who'd been leftist Iranian revolutionaries in the late 1960s, radicalized at the University of California. Throughout my life, my mother told stories of Berkeley smoldering after protests and the chemical bite of tear gas. But I was born in 1979 and grew up in the suburbs of Washington, DC. My personal experience with protest movements and revolt was largely gleaned from these stories and history books.

When I had started reporting and researching this book in 2013, I thought I was trying to answer questions my parents left unanswered before they died: What was so important that it was worth risking their lives and then later, our family? How had their choices—decisions made long before I was born—actually shaped me and who I am, now that I am grown, and they are gone?

These aren't questions unique to me. We are all of us shaped by the families that raise us—as well as by the families that predate us. Their histories and expectations sometimes ground us, and often give us something to kick against as we figure out the threads in our story that are uniquely our own. I am a child of revolutionaries, activists, immigrants, refugees, and asylum seekers, and my family's history is woven tightly with the histories of two nations. By exploring my history, I've been forced to wrestle with my complicated feelings toward both places: Iran, the ancient homeland that executed my father and expelled my family, and the United States, a country built on slavery and racism that took my family in, giving us asylum and refuge so we could thrive.

This year, 2020, was my fortieth, which also means that it's been more than forty years since the Iranian Revolution. Thirty-seven years since my father's death and ten years since my mother's, a span of time without them that, at its start, seemed unfathomable.

This year was also when, while covering the protests, I started feeling cramps late at night. For a week, I was kept up by the pain, curled into a fetal position on the couch with my eyes screwed shut. The deep ache wasn't going away and my period hadn't arrived.

Finally, about three in the morning after Independence Day, I shuffled to the bathroom and pulled out an old pregnancy test left over from before we'd known that the chance that I could get pregnant was almost nil.

Minutes passed.

I crawled into bed and ran my hand down my husband's back to wake him.

"I'm pregnant," I said.

And now seven months have passed, and in the interim I've reconsidered this book. It's no longer just an interrogation of history; it's also my own record of it. It's not just my effort to uncover why my parents chose the paths they did; it's also an exploration of how their choices influenced my own and of this question: How will my choices, made years ago, shape this new person about to be born?

This is a memoir of my parents. It is an examination of our personal and political history. But it is also my own meditation on how we continue like threads stitched across decades, connecting generations.

PART I

ONE

Tehran, Iran, 1982

On a humid July morning when I was nearly three years old, my mother and I said goodbye to my father at the threshold of the apartment and walked out onto the street. We didn't know it would be our last glimpse of him. I didn't know that, once the door closed behind me, my father would start to fade from my memory like smoke. Two hours later, not far from our home, he was arrested. When, sometime afterward, I asked where he was, my mother told me he had gone to Europe to finish his doctorate. It must have seemed to me that he had simply disappeared into air.

Until that moment, this is what I knew of life: my wants, my needs, and my actions would cause the world around me to expand or contract accordingly. I was rewarded when I was good and punished when I was bad. My parents came when I called. Now my father was gone, and I couldn't make sense of it. It felt like a punishment. Perhaps, I thought, I misbehaved one time too many.

Up till then, I had been fair with my parents. The two of them would sit together in our apartment—their backs against the wall, their knees pulled up to their chests—exchanging stories about their day, and I would toddle up, place one hand on my father's knee and the other on my mother's. I would give a kiss to one and then the other. Never one more than the other. After my father's disappearance, it seemed to me that I had been careless. One morning I had left my father behind, and he had been taken away. I watched my mother closely, worried she might follow.

A few weeks after he was taken from us, when my mother was seven months pregnant with my brother and desperate for space, she brought me to an aunt's house and told me that I would stay there with my cousins for a sleepover. A couple of days being cared for by a favorite relative probably felt to me like a respite from this new reality: a disappeared father, a terrified mother, and a lost home. Or perhaps all I could do was wait by the door for my mother's return.

After she left me with my aunt, my mother went back to one of the houses where we'd been hiding since my father's arrest. It was surrounded by a sprawling garden spread over several acres. At its far end, some way from the main house, a high wall separated the estate from Evin Prison, where my father was held.

That night my mother did not try to sleep. All the things she did not know and all the things she could not know stretched out in front of her into the darkness. She lay outside on a chaise and looked down the sloped grounds toward the prison. Hours passed before the sun rose over the sharp peaks of the Alborz Mountains. As the sky lightened, the large speakers that dotted the circumference of the prison switched on; for a moment the air seemed to crackle. The muezzin began the day's first call to prayer, his wail amplified so as to be heard in every prisoner's cell and inside the darkened bedrooms of the surrounding homes. It was loud enough that my mother could feel the chaise vibrate beneath her.

When the prayer faded, the prisoners answered: thousands of men and women bent forward, then sat back on their haunches, calling to God.

My mother did not pray; she stared ahead, exhausted. Her brown eyes were rimmed red behind her thick glasses. She was trying to decide if she and I should leave Tehran for California, where her mother lived and where she herself had lived for most of her life. She did not want to leave Iran; she wanted to stay close to my father and give birth to my brother in her homeland.

But it was becoming more difficult to find a place where we could stay for more than a few days at a time. We had been in hiding for weeks, moving between the homes of family members, friends, acquaintances, and in this case, a near stranger. They had taken us in at huge risk to themselves; many were afraid to do so again. My mother had put off making a decision and her belly had grown wide and heavy. If we were to leave Iran before my brother was born, we'd have to go in the next few days.

My mother got to her feet and picked her way across the lawn, past the gnarled oak tree and across the small stream that snaked over the garden's surface. As she made her way toward the wall, the prayers became louder. The noise pushed past the stone and filled the space around her body. She walked the wall's length slowly, concentrating on the voices a thousand feet from her.

Their prayers ended, and the prisoners began to chant fidelity to Ayatollah Khomeini. "Imam Khomeini," their voices called out, "to pay for our crimes, we have to become a wall protecting the fighters at the front. Down with the US . . . with the help of God's party, the prison has become a university. Imam Khomeini, God be with you. We don't have anything against you in our hearts . . ."

My mother listened to the prisoners and tried to pick out the voice of any one of her friends who were imprisoned in Evin. They must be there, she thought, among the chorus. They must be. She wouldn't think about where else they might have been held or what else could have been happening to them. As the voices began to fade, she strained to pick out the voice that mattered most: she listened for my father.

She sat down on the ground, her back pushed against the wall, and tried to hear him. She talked to him as if he were sitting next to her, like it had been when they were home together. This had become her ritual. Five times each day, as the prisoners were called to prayer, my mother turned her attention to them for a few moments. She didn't know exactly where my father was being held, but she believed he was somewhere on the other side of the barrier, his deep voice mixing with the prayerful.

She couldn't have known he was in a cell beneath the prison complex. His enclosure was likely section 209, a group of cells that had been built above the interrogation chambers during the shah's reign. These rooms have been described as narrow with a fingernail sliver of glass high on one wall. This was where, in a prison full of political prisoners, they kept those at the highest level. It was a prison within the prison, built at the foot of the mountain, and it stretched several stories underground.

Deep into the night, as the interrogators whipped the soles of prisoners' feet with wire cables, all of the prisoners in section 209 would have heard the screams. The cries of pain punctuated by moments of quiet. In the pauses, my father would've listened as air filled his lungs and followed the sound as he expelled the air from his nostrils.

My mother couldn't have known that his voice was too far buried to reach her in the garden. Nor that while she walked beside the garden's wall, my father was likely in his cell believing we were far away, on our way to California. Or perhaps he thought we had already arrived there, in the place where he and she had met and planned a revolution.

He didn't know she was still making her choice.

~

Washington, DC, 2010

I was in the living room in my mother's house, bent over her body, which was stretched out on the bed that hospice had set up the week before. Ameh[1], my father's youngest sister, was next to me. My mother's breathing slowed to a stop. More than a minute passed, but I kept listening. I wanted to make sure the last exhale we'd heard was, in fact, her last. I must have looked at a clock because I remember it was 2:43 a.m. when she died.

Hours later, I was back in the same room, looking through the glass doors as the sun rose over the high-walled garden that was carefully landscaped with pink, white, red, purple, and yellow blossoms—brilliance contained. My twenty-seven-year-old brother, Nema, sat next to me on the couch. Our family—my stepfather, two uncles, and aunt—had gathered, and we moved as if trapped in a loop between the living room and the kitchen. The sliding doors that separated the living room from the outside stood ten feet high and stretched the length of the room. At different times throughout the morning, when one of us felt cramped, we pulled hard against the heavy doors and stepped out for air. When we returned inside, we remarked how well the garden looked. It had never been more beautiful.

Just after sunrise, a short-haired woman came and took my mother's body to the crematorium. Soon, everyone else left, too. I sat outside with my brother and tried to remember the plant names our mother had told us the week before, when the three of us had been sitting in the same place.

That day, Nema—dark, compact, brooding, like the hero of a Brontë novel—had asked our mother about the plants. She lifted her head in a slow, concentrated movement. She raised her hand to her cheek and her eyelids moved, up and down, over unfocused brown

---

1   *Ameh* means paternal aunt.

eyes. We should have told her it didn't matter if she remembered the names, that we wouldn't remember them after she was gone anyway. I've forgotten everything my mother struggled to remember that day, but the image of the three of us sitting together, our faces warmed by the sun, remains.

~

Life continued. I moved out of my mother's home into my own in another part of Washington, DC. My stepfather sold their house that had too many stairs for an aging man and moved to an apartment outside the city, while my brother moved down to Richmond, Virginia, for work.

A year passed. I accepted a position as a columnist covering Capitol Hill and the US Congress. My brother's work took him to Pittsburgh, a few hours northwest. My stepfather fell in love. I felt relieved.

Another year went by. I was still writing one political story after another. My brother went to London for graduate school, then to San Francisco. I drifted away from my stepfather and his family. My friends got married. Some had first babies, others had a second. It seemed like all the lives around me were moving forward, while mine stayed still.

I stopped sleeping. I worked ten-to-twelve-hour days, and most nights I attended formal dinners with people who were sources, not friends. I breathed through one panic attack after another. For six months, I was covered from scalp to soles in unexplained inch-long welts. I would cry, paint myself with calamine lotion, and stay up late staring at my bank account and researching vacation rentals in Italy and France.

I missed my mother. I *missed* her. I missed taking care of her. I missed the reality of her. With only Congress and deadlines dictating my time, what was there for me? I was without her and I didn't know who I was without her.

One afternoon, Taylor, one of my best friends since high school, called from Vermont. We'd seen each other through long-distance moves, deep heartbreaks, and losing parents—his father and my mother. Now I told him about the sleepless nights. He reminded me that his family had a lake house in Quebec's Eastern Townships, just over the Vermont border. He said it would be empty for most of the summer and I could stay as long as I needed.

That was the first of May; by mid-June, my car was packed and my mother's three-year-old dog was in the passenger seat. My mother had begged my stepfather to let her adopt the funny, fluffy Havanese runt a couple of months before she started hospice—five years after she was first diagnosed with ovarian cancer. After my stepfather relented, Mom and I talked about names for days, before I suggested Huckleberry Finn and she agreed.

Now, Huck waited for me to start the engine before jumping on my lap and sticking his head out the open window. I turned over the engine and took my time driving north, stopping to visit friends along the way.

Four days after I left DC, I arrived in Quebec, passing green, rolling hills brushed over with wildflowers and dotted with great bales of hay. Cattle and sheep wandered the fields freely or dozed beneath the long, shady canopies of trees. At this point, the directions to the cabin became vague—*turn right after the general store, and then right, and then left again at the bottom of the hill*—but the dog and I found the house easily enough.

It was made of wood and stone, built on top of a steep hill face. The door was locked, and because my friend had lost the cabin's key, he had told me how to jimmy my way inside. I pushed at a splintering window frame until it gave, then hoisted myself over the sill. Old paint chips floated around my face as I tumbled onto the musty carpet.

I am safe, I thought, as I peeled myself off the floor.

~

My first day cut off from the world, like the days and weeks that followed, was filled with reading thick novels, swatting at fat mosquitoes, and falling into catnaps on the sun-streaked dock. Laziness replaced deadlines, politicians, and endless cigarettes. As a storm rolled in that first afternoon, I walked the ascent from the lake to the cabin and prepared a simple dinner from ingredients—chicken, asparagus, basil, sweet lettuce, and rosemary—I'd bought at the general store. I roasted the tender young chicken in the old oven and when it was done, the flesh fell from the bone. I plated my dinner carefully, tore off the end of a warmed baguette, and brought it out to the picnic table on the porch. While I ate, I looked down through the leaves to the lake below. Afterward, I watched an old black-and-white movie, sipped cold red wine, and nibbled chunks of dark chocolate. Then I cleaned the kitchen, took the dog out, and went upstairs to bed.

Days continued like this, one bleeding into the next. As soon as the first week by the lake ended, my memories started to rise up. I began to remember moments I hadn't thought about in years. Something inside me had started to loosen. Memories presented themselves and moved on, as if part of a roll call. They passed by like clouds over a blue sky. I watched them go.

Then one evening I took out a photo album I had brought with me to the cabin. I had thought it held pictures from the night before our escape from Iran. I expected to see images of my mother and uncle kneeling on the floor, peering into an open suitcase with clothes spilling out over the sides. But when I opened the album, I found that it was a different one.

This album was filled with pictures and newspaper clippings that chronicled my father's trial, sentencing, and funeral. Among these photographs was a black-and-white picture of my father and his father sitting together at a table somewhere in Evin, that infamous prison in

northern Tehran where my father and other political prisoners spent
their last months. In the photograph, my father's body is angled toward
my grandfather, but he's not looking at him. The camera captures my
grandfather's face as he breaks apart. My father would soon be sen-
tenced to death. This would be their goodbye.

I flipped through the rest of the album quickly. When I reached
the end, I noticed an orange compact disc tucked into the binder's
pocket. It was a copy of my mother's interview for the audio storytelling program *StoryCorps*, conducted when the program was collecting people's migration stories. On the CD sleeve was a line that
said "Storyteller," beside which my mother had written her name in
black ink. Below that, the interviewer had put down the date of the
recording: July 26, 2008.

I had never heard this recording; I hadn't heard my mother's voice
in years. I took the disc out of the case and stared at it for a minute before returning it to the album. I tucked both away on a high
shelf. Then I took a beer from the fridge, put the dog on a lead, and
walked to the dock. The sun was setting. The dog barked and chased
dragonflies.

~

A month or so later, my time in Quebec was drawing to a close, so
one afternoon before dusk I sat down at my computer and pushed the
compact disc into its drive. It had been one hundred degrees and humid
for most of the day, but with the door open and the screen closed, a
steady breeze cooled the cabin. I stared at the monitor and waited. The
disc whirred, and my mother's voice filled the room.

I closed my eyes as she told the story of leaving Iran for California,
a journey she made twice in her life. The first time in 1958, when she
was ten years old, and came to the United States to join her mother

in San Francisco. Five years later, my mother was naturalized as an American citizen.

The second migration happened in 1982, when she fled Iran at thirty-four, pregnant with my brother and saddled with me. I had heard versions of these stories countless times, so I ignored the details and concentrated on the sound of her voice.

How can I explain what it meant to hear a voice that was once so familiar and so loved, and for much of my life, so woven into my every day? I knew she was dead—I had tucked her ashes inside a sculpture of a plump bird and placed it on a shelf. But somehow when her voice came through the computer speaker, I got lost in the tone and cadence that were my mother's alone—it felt, almost, as if she were in the room again with me.

Minutes passed. Then the interviewer asked, "If your first husband were here today, what do you think he would think of your life now, in America?"

My mother paused.

"I think he would be very proud," she said.

A beat.

She began again, her voice low. "I think he would be very proud, because he would know how hard it was to get from where we were to where we are now."

Another pause. The dead air stretched out like limp elastic. I fingered the mouse pad to nudge the screen awake. The thin line at the bottom of the monitor tracked the seconds as they passed. Then my mother's voice began again, tight and controlled.

"My husband never saw his son," she said. "But his daughter, the apple of his eye—his ghost hovers over her."

I sat up, my back straight. I didn't know she knew about the ghost.

"It still does," she said. "They didn't see each other after my daughter was two and a half, but she longs for him, sometimes in a good way, sometimes in a heartbreaking way. My son longs for a father he never knew, but he isn't haunted like my daughter."

My mother paused. "I think, most of all, he would have been proud of his children."

The recording ended. I was alone in the cabin, both of my parents haunting me now.

TWO

Berkeley, California, 1969

This is how I imagine it happened: One warm September day lit by soft sunlight shining through the trees, casting patterns on the sidewalk, my father, Faramarz, and his roommate, Bijan, walked with their tennis rackets tucked under their arms. Their faces were dappled in light and shade as they turned onto Telegraph Avenue, the main drag connecting the city of Berkeley to its university.

They spoke to each other in rapid Persian and stepped around the young people slumped in doorways and nodding out against cars, these street kids who had followed the music and the dulcet promises of San Francisco and its Bay Area. These kids had come for a new way of life and found themselves mired in the dregs of utopia. Heroin and speed swept the area—there were no jobs or cheap housing in the city, so they'd moved here to the other side of the Bay, where at least it was warmer.

My father had rolled into Berkeley in 1967, during the summer of the year dubbed the "Summer of Love." He wasn't there for the music or the drugs; he didn't come to drop out or tune in. He was there for graduate school. He had chosen Berkeley because, tucked in and around the hippies, there were others like him, including a growing community of young Iranians.

He had spent the four years previous getting an engineering degree from a small college in Rolla, Missouri, a town smack in the middle of the United States. There, he'd spent many mornings completing military drills and marches as part of the curriculum. There, he'd been one of a few foreigners. But in Northern California, he was one of many. These foreign-born students hadn't come with their parents or grandparents. They had come to the United States to earn a college degree; they came alone or in pairs, and what a time it was, to settle in California, to study at Berkeley.

> Time it was
> And what a time it was
> It was a time of innocence,
> A time of confidences.[2]

When does a family begin? Is it when a child's heart begins to beat or when their mind comes alive; does it begin with the first child or the last sibling? Or does it begin years before, when one person finds another? Does the family emerge when two move toward each other, across time and space, like magnetized particles? Or is it more of a collision course: two comets hurtling toward each other and we, their children, are the explosion?

Did I begin, and for that matter, did my brother begin, the moment my mother and father met?

If the answer is yes, then an ordinary afternoon is important to me, to us, to this story.

If the answer is yes, then they were my parents even then—my mother and my father—though we wouldn't meet for another decade, when I would be born, screaming and defiant.

---

2 *Bookends.* Simon & Garfunkel. 1968.

Eleven years after immigrating to the United States to be with her mother, who'd immigrated following her divorce from my mother's father, my mother, Farahnaz, had moved to Berkeley from San Jose. It was May 1969, the weekend after Berkeley's Bloody Thursday protests. When she stepped onto Telegraph Avenue, she found that storefronts had been smashed in and cars overturned. The place was still smoking. Berkeley was under martial law and on a curfew. My mother took in the scene as she made her way down the street, holding a scrap of paper with an address scratched over its surface.

Berkeley wasn't the first city she had lived in that bore the scars of struggle between students and entrenched institutions. She had lived in Paris the year before, in the spring of 1968, during the seven weeks of unrest that started with more than one hundred people taking over a building to protest how the bureaucracy was underfunding the universities. The movement quickly grew into a stand against war, imperialism, and class division; it inspired workers' strikes, and police responded with tear gas and mass arrests. Campuses closed first, though eventually the whole city ground to a halt. Some people worried the upheaval could turn into civil war.

My mother lived in a cold, little room above an alley filled with garbage bins when the capital erupted and its schools closed. Unable to speak the language well and without classes to take up her days, she occupied herself by walking and watching students hoist placards into the air and shout slogans to the sky.

La beauté est dans la rue![3]

She watched their faces stretch and twist in anger. She was a witness; the fury wasn't hers.

---

3   Translates to "Beauty is in the street." Slogan printed on a poster from the 1968 Paris protests. I have a version of this poster tattooed on my left triceps.

My mother had imagined a different sort of Paris sojourn. One where she'd sit in a café, pattering in French, sloshing red wine over the lip of her glass, a cigarette held between two fingers, as she debated the merits of Camus and Sartre. Then again, my mother didn't care too much for philosophy, and her solitary life—staying in the small room heated by a wood stove—was remarkably romantic. It was a very John Keats existence and she adored Keats. She adored all the Romantics.

She slouched and frowned; she tried to read French newspapers as the city pulled itself apart around her. She loved great, fat nineteenth-century novels like *War and Peace* and *Les Misérables* and here she was living as if she were a minor character in one.

As the weeks passed, Paris began to thaw, and golden light sliced through the fast-moving clouds overhead. If my mother had looked past the masses packed together, screaming in the streets, then she might have glimpsed the two-thousand-year-old city beginning to bloom even as it was, once again, the backdrop for a new revolution: the movement was spreading across Europe and beyond.

A year later and half a world away, my mother was walking through Berkeley, as it, too, now buckled and clashed. This time, the upheaval meant something more to my mother than just literature and romance. She had grown up in Northern California and she was about to transfer into the jewel of the University of California system. It was her first day of apartment hunting, and the anger surrounding her—like the anger she'd witnessed in Paris—wasn't her own. Not yet.

My mother was excited to be at the university. She had grown up feeling isolated and deeply depressed at her high school in Monterey, a coastal town a couple of hours south of Berkeley, on California's central coast, and she'd left as soon as she could. She opted to finish her high school credits at the local community college before following her older sister, my Khaleh[4], and her brother-in-law to Colorado College, where they were teaching. Khaleh was seven years older than my mother and had immigrated to the States a year before her. Though they were close, the sisters hadn't really lived together since they were children.

In Colorado, my mother still felt ignored by her peers and set apart from college life. It was spring of her sophomore year that she went to Paris and then back to Iran for the summer, to visit her father.

If I were going to choose one moment when my mother stepped onto the path that would set the course for all that would come, it would be when she handed her passport to the man at passport control at the Tehran airport and he welcomed her home. He, a stranger, pronounced her name, *Farahnaz Ebrahimi*, easily. The sounds rolled from his tongue. His accent, perfect. It had been years—ten, exactly—since my mother recognized her name in a stranger's mouth. She felt her body exhale. It was as if she had been searching for a place where she belonged. Somewhere, she made sense. And that somewhere was Iran, back where she'd started.

By the end of the summer, my mother's broken Persian was stronger than it had been, though still rough. She had reconnected with her father and extended family—at least, they weren't strangers to her anymore. In her American home, she felt like an awkward, foreign thing; in Iran, though she wasn't perfectly Iranian, she felt a familiar pull. It was, if not home, then homelike. She felt like she had stepped into a moment of *déjà vu*, as if a word had finally been pulled from the tip of her tongue. She relaxed. She was where she wanted to be.

When it was time to leave, my mother knew what she wanted to do with the rest of her life. She'd go back to California, finish school as quickly as possible, get a master's, and then move to Iran to teach English. She got accepted into San Jose State for the fall term of '68 and into Berkeley for the following summer. The first day at San Jose, she

---

4   *Khaleh* means maternal aunt.

walked past a table of young Iranians eating lunch together. Many had recently come to the United States, but a few were like her—Iranians who had grown up in the States.

However alluring the scene was to her, my mother felt intimidated. Her family had warned her to stay away from Iranian students because they were usually political and said all sorts of treasonous things. Politics wasn't a game. It could be dangerous. It could invite danger.

But then again, these students were kids, sitting together on campus. In my mind, I see them all denim clad with long sideburns, laughing loudly and talking over one another as my mother walked by, stealing a glance over her shoulder. She said that like sirens they called out to her. They immediately adopted her as one of them. They accepted her as one of them.

Almost all of these Iranians became new fast friends, with each other and with her. Most were members of the local chapter of the Iranian Student Association, a campus group that upheld the time-honored tradition of foreigners who shared the same language, culture, and background banding together. The ISA, my mother quickly learned, could help connect members with anything: a job, an apartment, a roommate, and a tutor. They offered English classes for the new arrivals and Persian classes for those raised in the West. So when the time came for my mother to move to Berkeley, to find a place to live and a roommate to live with, the ISA helped her with that.

On that first day in Berkeley, she walked hurriedly down Telegraph Avenue. She had a quick, funny gait: heels in and toes out. It pitched her hips back and forth in a way that was a little tomboyish and a little suggestive. She found the sublet, which belonged to a young couple who were visiting Iran for a few months. The apartment was essentially a small room, but my mother took it to share with another Iranian girl I'll call Naz, who was a few years younger than she, the little sister of a friend.

The girls moved into the studio with a love seat, milk crates, a phone, and a turntable. They slapped fat psychedelic-flower decals on the walls and pulled down the Murphy bed to share. That summer, their apartment was where everyone gathered on their way to the Iran House, the meeting place for all the ISA chapters in Northern California, a couple of blocks away.

Do you remember falling for your friends?

Do you remember the rush of it?

The delight of it? The relief and the joy of it? The feeling was: *Of course! Of course!* The feeling was one of being found, finally. Found in a way that made you realize you had been lost, floating aimlessly in a too-big world.

The feeling was: *I'm not alone, not any longer. I am not a freak. I am accepted and I accept in return.*

Life became an exclamation point, the blood sang and the heart expanded.

So it was for my mother and so it was for my father—and so it would be for me.

When my mother found the ISA, the Iran House, and moved to Berkeley, she felt an acute sense of well-being, happiness, and complete fulfillment. For the first time in her life, she didn't feel depressed, quiet, and watchful. She felt exhilarated.

Months passed. It was now fall, the afternoon my parents met, when my father and Bijan were hoping for tennis, and my mother was in her apartment going about her day. She didn't know her next thing was coming.

My father was walking to her, probably taking all the political pamphlets handed to him along the way. He may have nodded to the people he recognized, on the street where she lived.

Bijan was good friends with my mother, new friends with her even though it felt as if they'd known each other for several lifetimes. He and she had talked about playing a match that day, so—*knock, knock,*

knock—he was there to collect her. Now my parents met formally, though they must have recognized each other from Iran House. They leaned in, a kiss on both cheeks in the Iranian way.

That afternoon, my father was wearing a light-yellow polo shirt.

He was in graduate school.

He had a kind American girlfriend with long, dark blond hair.

He was three years older than my mother.

He was intense, with a big laugh.

My mother later said that he wasn't tall, but he was broad and sturdy, built like a soccer player.

At that time, my mother still wore makeup.

She still ironed her tight, kinky curls, trying to force her natural Afro into straight locks.

Then, she wore her skirts short and jeans tight around her butt, flared below the knees.

She was quick-witted and warm. She had a full lower lip.

My mother put on a kettle for tea, or maybe she reached into the refrigerator for beer. The members of the ISA could still drink then. This would change over the next months when the ISA began to morph from a collective of young Iranians coming together for community into a collection of political factions whose leaders started to impose rules over how people should—and eventually how they could—behave.

The three of them talked. Perhaps one of them dropped a record on the turntable, a melodic backdrop to their conversation. They talked; the hours slipped away, and then somehow it was night. Too late for tennis, so perhaps they decided to stay at my mother's, and they made dinner and shared wine, or maybe they went out for burgers. They talked all night—not just my parents but Bijan, too—into the early hours of the next day.

After my mother died, I found a picture in her wallet of these friends, taken during those early months of their friendship. They're in someone's apartment; my father and Bijan are sitting next to each other in wooden-armed chairs with black leather cushions. They are both sporting sideburns. Bijan's head is tilted slightly back, while my father's chin is down so he is looking up at the camera. Both men are seated with their hands on their thighs. They aren't smiling, but their eyes are shining. My mother is standing between them; her hip is cocked slightly and her hand is on my father's chair. She's wearing a striped minidress with a crocheted belt and a long navy jacket. Her legs are tanned, and though she is petite, her legs are long. Her hair reaches below her shoulders. Her smile is warm.

They are perfectly young and beautiful. Other friends are around them, all smiling or about to speak. My mother's roommate, Naz, is standing toward the back; her hair is twisted up in a chignon, and she is halfway through a laugh.

What does it mean that this is one of the pictures my mother carried in her wallet? What does it mean that she took it with her everywhere until the day she died?

THREE

Tehran, Iran, 1963

I've often tried to imagine my father at eighteen, but I can't seem to, so instead I think of my brother at the same age and project my father's face onto his. The two look alike, except for the eyes—my father had green like mine, and my brother has brown like my mother's. My father had a long and oval face as a teen, though by his thirties, the bones and muscles broadened and fixed themselves in place. He had a smattering of acne scars along his cheekbones and a pair of piercing eyes set close to a long, straight nose. He wore his dark hair close on the sides and full on top, arranged into a little swirl at the hairline. When he smiled, two deep dimples appeared.

In Tehran, my father lived in a large house with his parents and three siblings, on the third alley off Taghavi Street. Both the street and its seven alleys were named for my great-grandfather, the merchant Mohammad Taghavi. These byways branched out from the main street like offspring in a line: 1 Taghavi Alley, 2 Taghavi Alley, 3 Taghavi Alley, and so on. Three Taghavi, where my father lived, was divided: on one side the families were wealthy and on the other, less so. Some of the homes had a front garden but both sides had a garden in the back, each with a small pond filled with orange goldfish. On many mornings, the alley's residents, rich and poor, would lay down Persian carpets around the pools and carry out samovars of hot black tea, which they poured in delicate glass cups. They dipped sugar cubes into the hot liquid to suck out the sweetness. They ate a breakfast of warm bread and freshly cracked walnuts with salty feta cheese, and an assortment of jams, marmalades, and honey, with views of the mountains around them.

In later years my father's little brother, my Amu[5], told my brother, cousins, and me stories about those days while tucking us into bed during the summer weeks we'd stay with him. I was the oldest of the American cousins, and as the others fell asleep, I held on to the images my uncle's tales conjured for me. I saw the Taghavi streets overflowing with families, each one with children, kids of all ages. Half were related or had known each other long enough to feel like blood. Everyone there was off together having adventures, while I was stuck in boring real life.

My father, his older brother, Farid, their cousin, and my father's best friend, Rostam, were together all day and stayed at each other's houses most nights. The four of them raced around their neighborhood on bikes, slingshots sticking out of their back pockets. Afternoons were for playing soccer. If neighborhood kids stole the ball from them or if they tried to cheat in pickup games, my father would be furious. He believed in honor among thieves and children. If he caught anyone breaking this code, he'd, inevitably, start a brawl. His older brother, a natural negotiator, would step in to smooth out the disagreement, or failing that, help my father win his fight.

Most days, my father would leave the school building, shoving his books down the front of his pants to keep his hands free for a fist fight, a bike ride, or a tree climb. He and the others would scale the wall to his grandfather Taghavi's garden, which had acres of fig, pomegranate, and pistachio and trees full of ripe, sweet mulberries and honeysuckle bushes. There, the boys ate their fill and then took out their slingshots to aim at the birds settled on branches. They'd let the rocks fly and the

---

5   *Amu* means paternal uncle.

small creatures, sparrows usually, fell to the ground. The boys picked up the dead birds, plucked their feathers, and roasted the carcasses over small fires. They'd eat the fowl, spit out the thin bones, and lick their fingers.

Amu tried to follow the older boys, who were fast and sure-footed as they moved around the neighborhood, quick as anything. Amu begged to be given a go at the slingshot or a taste of the tiny birds. His brothers, so much older than he, ignored him or waved him off, to go home to be dressed like a doll by his older sister and cousins.

I didn't realize when I was small and reveled in these tales that the stories were teaching me about where I came from, and about human complexity and internal contradictions. The father I met in the story world was alternately a bully and the platonic ideal of the mischievous boy. He was often the child most virtuous, sometimes taking the money his father gave him to pay for his school tuition to cover a less fortunate friend's. He threw punches at kids who slurred a friend's religion or family. What I learned was, my father was principled. He was brilliant, artistic, and precise. He was also impatient, rigid, and short-tempered. He ignored people he didn't care for, be they children or adults, yet when he loved someone, he was their champion.

The night before my father left Iran for Missouri, Rostam slept over, as he did almost every night. Until then, if the two were apart for even a day, they felt as if they had been away from each other for a year.

Rostam cried when he realized this would be their goodbye.

But my father didn't. He was on the cusp of his first great adventure. Who knew what would be waiting for him beyond their neighborhood, city, and country?

Neither young man knew then how cyclical life can be. And how could they? The less a person says *goodbye*, the more *goodbye* feels like a permanent fissure. It was unimaginable that night that they would see each other again. It was unimaginable that they wouldn't be living the life they had until then.

They didn't know this: they'd spend the next four summers together waiting tables at a restaurant in a town north of New York City, and they would do that every summer until my father left Rolla for Berkeley. In New York, Rostam would work his way up from the back of the kitchen, washing dishes, to the front of the restaurant. He would save his money and put himself through university. He knew he wanted to own a business; he knew he wanted it to succeed. He wanted the American Dream—financial stability and professional success. During these hot months, my father would grow more and more concerned about issues of justice—more skeptical about making money for its own sake. He would worry for the young Iranians who came to the United States without jobs, money, or much of a sense of how to get by in a strange, foreign land.

But all that was still in the future.

Leave-taking highlights differences between people, otherwise easily ignored. In the case of my father and Rostam, one was leaving; the other was being left. My father could fly off and feel confident in his future. His family could support him. It was his family after all who built the neighborhood where they both lived; it was Rostam's family who lived on the other side of the street, where people had less. Rostam was also Jewish in a Muslim country; my father was raised Muslim. It would never again be as it was on the night the two friends said goodbye.

Though, five decades later, as I sat on his couch with my feet tucked beneath me, Rostam told me that no matter how far apart their lives took them, they loved each other as if they were blood brothers, always.

In a way, that last night in Tehran was a real goodbye: goodbye to their young boy selves. They'd never be so young, and the world could never hold such promise and such a variety of opportunities as it did for them then. The next day, they'd start moving in opposite directions, they'd make different decisions and those decisions would close some doors, even as they opened others.

~

Missouri, June 2018

I woke before dawn and boarded a plane that lofted through the air from New York City to land in Saint Louis. The first time I walk through an airport in a city, state, or country I've never visited before, I notice the image the region chooses to project of itself: the slogans on the walls, the souvenirs in the shops. I watch the people who fill the narrow terminals as they stare blankly at the rows of fridges stocked with the premade sandwiches or as they kill hours sitting at the bar, staring at television screens. I notice the slope of their shoulders as they slump uncomfortably into black plastic seats with shiny metal armrests. The people all look like each other, or rather, they look as if they belong together. They wear the same clothes and they wear their clothes the same way. They pull down the same hats manufactured by the same brands. They have the same manners and the same laugh. They use matching luggage.

During all my years waiting in and walking through airports, I learned to pay attention to the people who are a terminal's majority. When I do, I have a clue about what's waiting for me on the other side of the exit doors.

That morning in Saint Louis, as I jerked my head around, searching for hints that I was walking in the direction of the car rental offices, I saw a storefront with a counter decorated with small POW/MIA flags and lined with brochures trumpeting support for American troops. The sign above the counter claimed it was a "free-speech booth." Standing next to it was a big-bellied man with unkempt gray hair. He was wearing a T-shirt and glasses. I caught his eye and began to walk toward him. Why would someone need a space in an airport to share their views on anything but travel? And whose speech was projected or protected here?

The man watched me. I thought he looked like he was bracing himself. Or perhaps no one had stopped to talk to him all morning and he was about to speak for the first time in hours.

"What is this?" I asked, gesturing to the sign overhead. "How does it work?"

I was smiling, but my tone sounded discordant to my own ear. I stretched my smile wider to compensate.

"You have to fill out a form," he said. "Tell them what you want to talk about and then you can stand here and talk about what you want."

He seemed uncomfortable. I opened my mouth to ask another question. Something like, *Who is* them? *Who gets to okay who can talk about what?* But I changed my mind, and asked him where the car rentals were.

His shoulders relaxed and he gave me directions.

Inside the rental car building, a woman was tapping on a computer behind the counter. I gave her my reservation number and she asked if I was here for vacation "or is it work?"

I wanted to lean toward her and say, *Well, actually, I'm here to find my father. I lost him thirty-five years ago.*

Out loud I said, "I'm here for work."

Once in the car, I typed in the address of the Super 8 hotel in Rolla where I would be staying for the next two nights. I had a plan for the afternoon. I would check in to the hotel by my father's alma mater, Missouri Science & Tech, then I would get back in the car and drive down Route 66 through the Mark Twain National Forest to the middle of the country—the single point around which all the people in the country pivot. There I would park and let America spin around me.

Information can change and shape how we understand the past, and that was why I had come to Missouri: to follow my father back through time, all the way to his first summer in his college town where he arrived in the summer of 1963. He would have turned nineteen that summer, in a small town deep in a part of the country where I'd never been and couldn't quite imagine. It was fifty-five years nearly to the week after my father had arrived in Missouri. Now I was walking behind him, trying to uncover his footprints so I could step inside them. He has been a dead man for most of my life. I was trying to understand how he got to be that way. I was trying to understand why he made the choices he made, choices that led to my life and his death.

The center of America, I believed, might teach me something about my country, myself, and my father. It would be the culmination of one journey and the commencement of another.

I made a right out of the rental car lot, and as the miles passed, it felt more and more as if I were driving to meet him. As if I could catch him hiding in the engineering lab or ducking into the library. Maybe if I caught him, I could tell him to be more careful, with himself and our future. I'd ask him to go more slowly through his next years.

After an hour on the road, I pulled into a rest stop on the side of the highway. I couldn't have said where I was. As I gathered my phone and purse, I saw an elderly man with long, gray hair hunched and smoking. When they turned, I realized the person was a woman. Next to her sat a man with a long, white beard, wearing gray pants and opaque sunglasses. He had a cigarette in his mouth. Next to him was another man, in his thirties, with a shaved head and a pink scalp. He looked like he had something black under his nails.

I pushed my sunglasses up my nose as I walked past the three, reminding myself that no one here knew that I was Iranian or from the Middle East, reminding myself that I clearly carried my own prejudices with me on this journey.

In the restroom, as I washed my hands, I saw a little girl, maybe eight or nine, reflected in the warped mirror. She was a skinny thing in jean shorts, wearing thick pink glasses that brought out the red of the rash on her face. I smiled at her and she walked out the door.

I realized she belonged to the three I had seen on my way to the bathroom. They were a family. The girl had made me see them that way.

When I told this story to my brother, he asked me why I had felt out of place.

"It's Missouri," he said, "not, you know, Japan." I started to tell him that I hadn't known what to expect after Ferguson, after the election, after some guy not far from where I was going was arrested for shooting two Indian men, killing one, because he thought they were Iranian.

"Wasn't that in Kansas?" Nema asked.

"Near Kansas City, I think," I said.

On the radio Loretta Lynn sang about Louisiana women and Mississippi men and I sang with her. In the rearview, I saw a steel-blue truck. I glanced at my phone. It didn't have bars. I turned up the music and slapped my hands against the wheel in time with the beat. I sang louder.

I thought of the two Indian men and how in my father's 1966 college yearbook they had labeled his hometown, Tehran, which was correct, but said his homeland was India, which was not. It seemed this Iran/India confusion had been long-lived in this part of the country.

Paul Simon came on the radio, but I wished it were Simon and Garfunkel and that they were searching for America, because it occurred to me that this was kind of what I was doing.

I didn't know what I would find in Missouri, in the Ozarks. My dog, Huck, was from this state. He and I had been connected from the day my mother brought him home and I raced from work, bent over his pen, and scooped him up. He was, I thought, so brave. My baby Huck ripped away from his family, put on a plane, and brought home to strangers.

That day at my mother's, I lay down and put the dog on my belly. "I'll make sure you're safe," I said.

But the truth was, the small dog had saved me. He'd stayed with me while she died, curled up on her pillow. Afterward, he curled into me at night and forced me to leave the house every morning to walk him. When I wanted to disappear, he pinned me to the land of the living.

Now, I wished he were with me on this road trip. But Huck was back in New York with my partner, pushing his body flush to the door, waiting for me to come home.

Plato, Missouri, population 109, was, as far as I knew, notable primarily for being identified as the population center of the United States, after the 2010 Census. That didn't mean it was the exact physical middle of the country, but it was the mean center: the moving point around which all the human beings living in this country were balanced. When the 2020 Census is tallied and we finish counting up the casualties of COVID-19, this national pinpoint may shift. But in 2018, this was our center.

As I drove through Plato, I saw a woman in a pink bathing suit mowing her lawn. Two towhead children were playing in the front yard. One screamed loudly, though if it was from pleasure or pain, I couldn't tell. I passed a new brick building, several stories tall, with shiny letters that announced itself to be Plato's community center-cum-elementary-middle-and-high-school. Then the road went on, but the town was over.

I turned the car around and pulled over on the shoulder. It had taken less than two minutes to drive through Plato. I didn't have cell reception and hadn't for over an hour, not since I'd seen that blue truck, the only other car on that ribbon of interstate leading me farther and farther into the country.

At the center of America, in the heart of the heartland, I was cut off from the rest of the world. I held my dead phone in my hand, and I watched as a tractor moved around a green field. I tried to feel the country spin around me, the millions of lives moving at their own speed, each on their own path, as if tracing the groove of their own record. All those different humans, humming their varied songs, telling their own stories, each crisscrossing, moving, shaping one another.

I rolled down the window and listened, but all I heard was the drone of the tractor. It had taken all morning to arrive, and for a moment, all the people in this country circled me as if I was a fine and sharp needle and they were trying to balance on my pointed edge.

Here in Missouri, I felt like Dorothy before she stepped out of the house that crushed the witch and started on her way back home. Before she, a patron saint of refugees and immigrants, could begin collecting the people and their stories that helped her on her way. Not so different, she and I. Here I was collecting evidence and stories. Here I was trying to find a way home—and by home what I meant was that feeling I belonged.

FOUR

San Francisco, California, 1958

My mother left Iran when she was ten years old, a bird-boned girl with large brown eyes. Someone—a flight attendant, perhaps—hung a card around her neck and fastened it with string. My mother couldn't read the English words printed on the page, but knew the card had her name on it—Farahnaz—and the address where her mother lived in California. She traveled alone for three days, with stops in London and New York, before finally landing in San Francisco.

She waited for the flight attendant to come to her seat and walk her outside. My mother was nervous and a little afraid. The attendant walked her down the stairs from the plane to the tarmac; my mother looked all around her, searching the faces attached to tall bodies. Everyone was smiling and crying out to each other in a language she didn't know and had rarely heard.

My mother hadn't seen her mother since she was seven. Now she was ten, and seven felt like a lifetime ago—think of all the world absorbed at eight and nine. Seven is a kid; ten is double digits.

As the fog burned off the Bay, my mother saw a woman with softly curled brown hair, high, elegant cheekbones, bow-shaped lips, and almond eyes. She glimpsed a little mole below a perfectly arched brow. My mother ran to her and wrapped her arms around the woman's waist.

Maman! she cried. *Maman!*

Her mother existed. My mother could touch the exquisite reality of this one body, prized above all other bodies. She pushed her small face into the solid warmth of the other's belly.

When she looked up, her mother was looking down at her. My grandmother didn't recognize her child, not at first. She might have been shocked to have seen her youngest older. She might have, for a moment, recoiled at being claimed, once again, for someone else.

Here, in the person of her daughter, was proof that life goes on without you.

~

Have you heard this one? The proverb about the nail, the shoe, the horse, the rider, the message, the battle, and the kingdom?

It goes like this. Something like . . .

> Once a nail went missing, so everything else crumbled, until, finally, a kingdom was lost. And all for want of a nail.

It's an old story, told and penned before the theory of the butterfly that flapped its wings and caused a catastrophe on the other side of the world. This one, about the nail, is about how something negligible and seemingly insignificant can create a series of events, like dominos falling in a line. *First the nail is lost, then the kingdom follows.*

What the adage doesn't do, what it cannot do, is answer *why? Why* was the horse, the one in need of the nail, dressed and bridled? *Why* was the rider, who was meant to hoist herself on the horse, delivering a message? Why was the message composed and what did it say? And why, for God's sake, was the kingdom in danger to begin with?

There are stories tucked tightly between those lines.

As I followed my family's story, these stories I am laying down on these pages, I found moments when our tale became entangled in the grand sweep of history, the machinations of state leaders, and the push and pull of empires. Political divisiveness has always influenced the lives toiling within its orbit, but for the most part, people go on. They put their heads down and adapt to a world of shifting allegiances.

Some people, however, aren't content to let things be as they are. They feel an obligation, and they have the privilege of time and space to ruminate on the present and then heave themselves against the rock face of history, demanding the world take notice and then change. Some people reject how they're told they *should* live and behave; they push to be themselves.

When I try to get to *why* it all began for my family, I can only answer *because*—

Because America, its myth and reality, was presented as an option.

My family's American story began with my maternal grandmother leaving her husband and bringing her children to the States in the mid-1950s, and it continued with my father's immigration in the early 1960s, later followed by his siblings. My mother and I returned to the United States from Iran in the 1980s because we needed refuge and a future. My family spent thirty years moving back and forth between these two countries: Iran, our ancient homeland, and the United States, our future homeland.

America was a promise. First, it gave us the chance to learn, then to develop, and finally, for us to lay claim. The door to America opened for my family when the United States entered Iran and began messing in the political system.

It started with a coup and a man who is nothing and nobody to me.

~

Tehran, Iran, 1953

The American James Lochridge arrived in Tehran in the middle of July. He was a nondescript young man with brown hair and horn-rimmed glasses, and he spent nearly every afternoon at the tennis court, challenging whoever happened to be looking for a match. Within a few weeks, he was adopted into the city's sparkling expatriate scene.

But he wasn't who he said he was. Lochridge was Kermit "Kim" Roosevelt Jr., the grandson of President Theodore Roosevelt and a distant cousin of President Franklin Delano Roosevelt. Kermit Roosevelt's version of things places him at the center of the key political events that were happening in that time and place; much of his story is disputed by scholars and it's important to acknowledge that he had a penchant for self-aggrandizement and cinematic storytelling, a genius for creating elaborate tales and telling them with great conviction. In short, he was the perfect spy to help pull off America's first coup d'état: Operation Ajax.

By the time Kim Roosevelt tiptoed over the Iraq border into Iran, he was already a hugely influential senior covert operative in the CIA's Near East and North Africa unit. He had a vision for the United States' role in the oil-rich region, a vision that had, in part, grown out of his devotion to writer and diplomat T. E. Lawrence and journalist Rudyard Kipling, from whose novel *Kim* he'd derived his own nickname.

His vision helped drive the American Arabist strategy, of which Kim was one of the major evangelists. At the end of the European theater of the Second World War, the Arabists wanted the United States to wrest control of the region's petroleum resources, then controlled by Great Britain and Europe. Arabists were, by and large, against the Jewish state of Israel and they believed that British and European influence in the region had atrophied to such an extent that it left the region vulnerable to Soviet influence. The US strategy to "contain" the power of Communist nations meant inserting itself into governments and countries they felt were vulnerable to Communism.

This is where Kim Roosevelt came in. Between 1948 and 1951, he helped to found three US-based Arabist propaganda groups that pushed good relations with Iran and Arab countries. One of these groups, the American Friends of the Middle East, was funded, in part, by Kim's own CIA.

The seeds for making the United States a dominant force in the region had been planted decades earlier. In 1933, the British state–owned Anglo-Iranian Oil Company had signed a treaty with Iran that gave Britain access to oil and profits from Iran's petroleum and promised control over Iran's oil reserves for sixty years. The deal was signed by the first Pahlavi monarch, Reza Shah Pahlavi, a former soldier who came into power through a 1921 coup d'état.

Two decades later, under the reign of the Pahlavi scion Mohammad Reza Shah, Iran's legislature voted to nationalize its oil, reneging on the agreement with Great Britain. Shortly afterward, a popular new prime minister, Dr. Mohammad Mossadegh, pushed through a series of laws that weakened the power of the shah and strengthened his plan to take over the Anglo-Iranian Oil Company's property in Iran. No nation, he said, could ever be truly independent without economic freedom. He believed that Iran would never be able to tackle major issues like poverty, justice, health, and education without also gaining complete independent control over the country's major natural resource.

Great Britain went straight to the newly formed International Court of Justice to sue Iran. The United States, which had been neutral, tried to broker a deal that would call for Britain to accept nationalized Iranian oil and for Iran to allow Britain to control drilling and production. Negotiations continued through most of 1952 under the Truman administration.

Then, in November, the Republican war hero Dwight D. Eisenhower was elected president, and US foreign policy focused on strict containment efforts that would stop Russia's "expansive tendencies" and check growing Soviet influence wherever it popped up around the world. This was the dawn of the Cold War.

Eisenhower's administration believed that Iran was vulnerable to Soviet influence, in part because Mossadegh's goal of nationalizing Iran's resources relied on a political coalition that included the country's Communist Party.

In the early months of 1953, Secretary of State John Foster Dulles approved plans for Mossadegh to be removed from power. His brother, CIA Director Allen Dulles, earmarked $1 million "to be used in any way that would bring about the fall of Mossadegh."[6]

It was time to act. The new Central Intelligence Agency, just six years old, was eager to prove itself.

By the summer of 1953, in an attempt to exploit the schisms in Mossadegh's coalition government, British and American spies, including Kim Roosevelt, paid members of the parliament, the military, the editors and publishers of newspapers, and influential religious leaders to say that Mossadegh's government was becoming despotic.

The coup was planned for August 15, 1953. An officer was supposed to arrive at Mossadegh's house at midnight to deliver an order, signed by the newly exiled shah, firing the prime minister. Once Mossadegh resisted, the officer could arrest him. A general loyal to the shah would be installed as the next prime minister and the shah, who still had allies in the military, would return with his power fully restored.

---

6   "Secrets of History: The C.I.A. in Iran—A Special Report. How a Plot Convulsed Iran in '53 (and in '79)." *New York Times*, April 16, 2001. https://www.nytimes.com/2000/04/16/world/secrets-history-cia-iran-special-report-plot-convulsed-iran-53-79.html

The shah, however, was nervous about signing off on the plan. If the coup failed, he worried he might lose his throne forever. He hesitated, and that pause gave Mossadegh's sympathizers enough time to warn the prime minister about what was coming. By the time the officer arrived with the shah's order in hand, Mossadegh had escaped.

The CIA declared Operation Ajax a failure and ordered Roosevelt to leave Iran; Kim thought he was a Kipling hero. Heroes didn't kowtow to fate, so neither would he. Armed with American dollars and British sterling, Kim re-upped his efforts to pay disgruntled Iranians to flood the Tehran streets and chant anti-government slogans. Then, he paid the police and military to confront the activists. Days of chaotic demonstrations followed, culminating in a gunfight in front of the prime minister's home. Hundreds were killed in the tumult.

The elderly Mossadegh, who had returned to his house, was again forced to run. He went over the wall of his garden and hid for a day before he was found and arrested. General Fazlollah Zahedi was appointed the new prime minister.

Within days of taking office, Zahedi undid all Mossadegh's policies. The shah came back and entered into a deal with the United States and Great Britain that gave them control over Iranian oil reserves. In exchange, Great Britain dropped the oil boycott they had started in 1951. The United States was invited to have a military presence in the country, and the Eisenhower administration solidified the new alliance by giving Iran aid—$5 million was given over immediately.

This was just the beginning. Over the next three decades, the US government trained thousands of Iranian soldiers, provided military aid and weapons, and shared CIA resources and expertise to help build the shah's secret police, SAVAK.

Running parallel to all of this was soft diplomacy, which meant bringing young Iranians to the United States to study. All at once, the number of cultural exchange programs between the United States and Iran and the number of student visas available to Iranians grew and became somewhat easier to come by, which finally brings us back to my family.

~

Iran to America, 1955

It wasn't too many years after the coup that my maternal grandmother, Ferdows, boarded a ship to bring her over the Atlantic to New York City, holding a student visa. From New York, she rode a train across the country to California to finish the college degree she'd started more than a decade earlier. She had been one of the first three women ever admitted to the University of Tehran, but she dropped out after she accepted my grandfather's marriage proposal.

My grandfather, Majid Khan, was Paris-educated and honey-tongued. His family owned hundreds and hundreds of hectares in Kerman, the same place where my grandmother had been born and raised. His family was one of the most powerful in the desert town; they even controlled the water. Ferdows was eighteen when they married. She was the only daughter of a Baha'i seamstress with an improbable opportunity to be the lady of the manor—a queen of the desert.

Years passed. The couple was glamorous and beautiful. They had three children in three-year spurts: the eldest, Khaleh, the middle, Daii[7], a boy, and the youngest, my mother, Farahnaz. More years passed, and the couple grew apart and increasingly unhappy until Ferdows decided she wanted something else. She left. My grandfather soon remarried, but my grandmother left her children with her mother and set off for California. It was the mid-1950s, she was thirty-nothing and ready for the next chapter of her life to begin.

---

7   *Daii* means maternal uncle.

When she arrived in America, she changed her name to Fay. She found an apartment in San Francisco and a roommate. She finished her undergraduate degree and began her graduate work in English. For a time, she worked in a factory pitting peaches. She made friends and went on dates.

After a year, she sent for Khaleh, her eldest child. Another year passed and she sent for my mother, her youngest. And then another year and she sent for her son, Daii. My grandmother was continuing a family tradition: she was the third generation of single mothers. The women on this side of the family worked to support themselves, their ambitions, and their children.

~

Semnan, Iran, 1920s

In 1921, the first monarch of the new royal line, Reza Shah, had a vision for modernizing and secularizing Iran. He wanted Iran to be respected by Western powers—the ancient nation was to be held up for their admiration and approval.

Before the beginning of the new shah's reign, a law had been passed that required every Iranian to choose a surname. Before this, only the very upper classes had family names that conveyed their lineage from one generation to another. Reza Shah had chosen a name for himself and his family: Pahlavi. He asked his subjects to follow his example.

It was around this time when my paternal grandfather, Hussein, a young man who dreamed of being a doctor, lost his father to suicide. My great-grandfather painted his suicide note across the walls of their home. Hussein, then fourteen, was now the head of the family. He packed his dreams away in order to go west to Tehran in the hopes he'd quickly find work in the bustling capital some 215 miles away.

I choose to believe that my grandfather decided our name early on his trek across the rocky desert terrain. The air was bone-dry. It whipped moisture from his brow; dust and sand became lodged in his hair, the corners of his eyes, and the edges of his teeth. He was still a boy, grieving for his father and afraid of what was to come for his mother, his sisters, and himself. The fate of the family weighed on him as he moved steadily toward a city that must have felt impossibly far. So far, it may as well have been another world.

I can't know how many days he walked or whether he was able to catch a ride with those who were moving in his direction, but I hope he had help as he went along. I hope he was more excited than afraid.

It was before his muscles became used to the exercise and as his fair skin began to burn under the relentless glare of the sun that I imagine my grandfather chose our name. He was a thoughtful and deliberate soul; he may have spent days playing with various possibilities. He felt each syllable as it moved over the surface of his tongue. He considered them. Maybe he went back and forth between several names. As he walked, he could have strung the names together, turned them into a rhyme to test the cadence. Choosing may have helped ward off the tedium of walking, constantly walking, through the rough-hewn and neutral-colored landscape. Maybe the act served as a balm to the feeling of moving, placing one foot in front of the other over and over again, without the relief of arrival.

Common sense says my grandfather would have begun his days early while it was cool, and the sky was still dark. Desert mornings are miraculous: the light expands across the beige and muted blues, and a sweep of blues, pinks, and violets heralds the dawn. For a moment, every living surface quivers under droplets of dew; the sky ebbs from inky blue to azure, then an explosion of peaches and reds and ecstatic yellows. The morning celebrates the whole of the desert: the subtle greens and golds, the splashes of white and indigo. The night, which was dark, cold, and lonely, fades away; in its place is a celebration of having persevered.

But the respite between the cool night and the hot day is brief: my grandfather could have seen the jagged mountaintops surrounding him and listened to sounds of the desert as they alternately swelled and calmed. His back would've begun to warm as if there was a hand pressed against him, urging him westward.

He chose this name: Toloui, *of sunrise*, and attached it to Semnani, *of the city of Semnan*. We are a clan born of the sunrise over Semnan, the city where his family started. Our history is contained in these words. Our name holds poems, journey, elation, and grief. When I say it, I am telling the story of our ancestors. When my grandfather chose it, we began to be what we would become: a clan of wanderers and seekers, determined dreamers moving through a too-real world.

In America, the name my grandfather gifted us has been broken into pieces. Some of us claim the first half, Toloui, and others the second, Semnani. I try to be like the hyphen in my name and hold together both halves; I try to hold the stories.

FIVE

Rolla, Missouri, 2018

It was early summer, 1963, when my father walked onto the campus of what was then called the University of Missouri School of Mines and Metallurgy. It was early summer, 2018, when I stood in the middle of the street, staring at the house where he used to live. No one was home to let me see the inside.

I looked down and across the street, then I turned and walked toward campus the same way I thought my father would have—up the hill, over the railroad tracks, across the creek—to the Electrical Engineering building where most of his classes were held. I imagined his young body walking quickly in front of mine. His hand might be pushed into his trouser pocket. If he was nervous for an exam or a project or if he was angry, he would've bitten the flesh of his left pointer finger—a habit my mother and Ameh told me about, a habit I tried and failed to adopt when I was in middle school.

As I traced his young man's steps, I felt his older self walking next to me. I imagined we were together, and he was the age he would've been had he lived.

Neda, he'd say, and point as he talked, *this is where I studied; where I ate; where I played. There is the tree I napped against between classes.*

He'd smile and shake his head.

Had it been a real father-daughter exchange, I'd have rolled my eyes, sighed.

All right, old man, I'd say. *Let's keep it moving. It's almost lunch time.* He'd laugh and put his arm around my shoulder.

All right, all right, he'd say. *One more place and then we eat.*

At the Electrical Engineering building, I opened the same door my father would have and walked in. Summer classes started that day and I heard a professorial voice in the midst of a lecture. Old equipment, pulled from the labs and classrooms, was filling the hallways. I looked over decades of equipment: great big computers, hard drives, and exposed circuitry. I opened silver cabinets filled with wads of paper. I leafed through books the size of several dictionaries that trumpeted indecipherable (to me) instructions concerning electronics and engineering. In one classroom, I picked up a flyer that explained how to respond to an active shooter. Back when I graduated from college, mass shootings had been a rarity, not ubiquitous as they are now. I realized neither my father nor I would know what to do if an armed man came onto campus and started squeezing off bullets—one small thing we have in common.

I walked through the building slowly, taking time to look out of every window. These were the same hallways he wandered down, the same classrooms he walked into and out of. When I get to the labs in the basement, the doors are locked, but looking through the window, I can see it hadn't changed much from my father's days. One wall was lined with clamps, different-sized wrenches, and handsaws. I could see metal shavings on one of the worktables. It was as if someone had stepped away but would return at any moment.

I was, I realized, moving through a palimpsest, which is the kind of word a person searches for the first time they use an eraser to wipe away a pencil mark. Palimpsest is the slightly visible remnant of something erased. It's the word one needs when sitting down for dinner the night after someone they love has gone away. It is the past we try to rub out but are forced to contend with. It is a glimpse of the world as it used to be and a reminder of how far we've come toward the future. Palimpsest is the faded sign visible on the side of an old building. It is the past mixing and meshing with the present.

No one knows much about my father's life in Rolla, a small town that, according to the school's archivists, didn't experience the sixties like the rest of the country. What happened to my father here to have made him curious about the scene in Northern California? Something must have happened in these halls, on these grounds, that made my father choose Berkeley, and politics, and activism.

But I'll never find it, because what I know about my father, I've stitched together from scraps of other people's memories. From stories I've heard, I can picture him as a child shooting birds or as a man watching cartoons with my mother. I've been told he laughed with his head thrown back. But what I have from him are his sketches and artwork, his master's thesis, his voice singing on a record, a video and transcript of his trial, school report cards and yearbooks, and his last letter.

I spread out all of this as if it were fabric. I arranged and rearranged these fragments so that they could amount to something.

~

Northern California, 1970

Nineteen sixty-nine ended and the winter rains gave way to the lush greens of California springtime. The air was fresh, the afternoons were warm, and my mother, father, and Bijan were together nearly every day. They'd sit together on one of the campus lawns, making picnics on weekday afternoons as friends came and went.

My parents weren't hippies. Emphatically, they were not, and neither were their people. The "turn on, tune in, drop out" scene was old and from the previous decade. In their opinion, that scene was bullshit.

This was a new decade. These weren't la-di-dah meetings; everyone was coming from a protest or going toward one. They were always talking, arguing, laughing, fighting, and planning. Planning. Always planning.

If something needs changing in this world, if wrongs need to be made right, then take on the responsibility and change it, they thought. *Don't move away in frustration, hiding in drugs and music, trying to numb yourself. Immerse yourself in action. Be principled and focused. Nothing can matter more than trying to change everything.*

Nearly every day protesters and police clashed on the streets. It seemed the university was closed more than it was open. Later, my mother's descriptions of her Berkeley years included enormous demonstrations with thousands of people on the streets, a radicalized student movement, the Chicago Seven and the Students for a Democratic Society (SDS), Tom Hayden, and Abbie Hoffman.

Among the American student groups, the SDS had splintered and morphed into several political factions, including the Revolutionary Union, which became the New Communist Organization. Further on the fringe, the Weather Underground Organization was becoming increasingly radical. As the far left became more militant, the anti-war movement and the counterculture moved into the mainstream. Iranian students started to create parallels between what they were doing and what the radical American and European student groups were doing.

Tuesday nights, my parents walked from their respective apartments or from campus to Iran House, the meeting place for all the Iranian Student Association chapters in Northern California. They'd skirt the perimeter of the church near the corner of Dwight Way and Hillegass Avenue, across from People's Park. Singly or with small groups, they entered a large room furnished with bookshelves stuffed haphazardly with volumes and pamphlets stacked messily one on top of the other. There was a ping-pong table and chairs that could be moved or folded away, depending on how many were attending the meeting.

Tuesday nights were for learning, for sharing, for being around others who spoke the same language, understood the same references, and knew the same music. If a young Iranian was far away from home and felt alone and misunderstood, if they were tired of speaking a foreign language and hearing a different cadence, then here was a place to go. At Iran House, students didn't have to be lonesome anymore. Here, people were waiting for them. Here, they belonged.

The ISA had begun years before as part of the American Friends of the Middle East, that CIA-funded group co-founded by Kim Roosevelt. But by the 1960s, as the Iranian students became more critical of the shah and his government's relationship with the United States, the ISA broke away from the AFME.

Around the same time, another organization was forming. Iranian students studying in Germany, France, and England came together in Heidelberg, Germany, and formed the Confederation of Iranian Students in Europe. In 1962, the CIS, the ISA, and the student organizations at Tehran University in Iran combined to form the Confederation of Iranian Students, National Union, affectionately referred to among its members as the Confederation.

The Confederation was a transnational organization with branches throughout the United States, Europe, and Iran. Its early constitution said it was "the corporate and political representative of Persian students at home and abroad." As the decade went on, the Confederation became more political and its focus shifted from representing Iranian students generally, to being an organization closely aligned with leftist groups.

But politics hadn't fully taken over the American ISA when my parents started attending Tuesday night meetings at Berkeley's Iran House. Back then, it didn't matter too much what a person believed: there were nonpolitical and religious students there, along with those who aligned with the National Front, Mossadegh's party—those less concerned with ideology and more concerned that Iran, specifically Iranians, hold sovereignty over their natural resources and their government.

Then there was the panoply of leftist student groups: those who sympathized with Castro's Cuban Revolution, others who held up the Bolsheviks as the gold standard, some who thought Stalinism had something to it, and others who thought Mao Zedong's Cultural Revolution was the way forward. And then there were those who picked through political ideologies as if they were at a buffet; they took a little from every theory to create a framework to suit how they saw the world. Many people weren't affiliated with any particular group at all.

Within the groups that met at Iran House, clandestine political factions were just starting to form. Their members tried to remain known only to one another. The secrecy was meant to protect themselves and their comrades from the FBI and the shah's SAVAK agents, who were trying to infiltrate the student movement.

A few blocks from the Iran House, in a small single-family home, several young men had begun getting together to discuss and dissect political theory. They began as a party of five, which included one young man I'll call Sharam and another I'll call Payam.

Sharam barely clears five feet, five inches. He walks quickly with confidence and has a wide gait like a horseman. His face is as round as the frames of his glasses. He laughs easily; he tells a good story. His voice is soft and scratchy at the edges, with a trace of a Persian accent, but as he grew up in California, it's faint and almost unplaceable.

I know this because I've known him most of my life, and while I was reporting this book, we spent days together talking and driving through Berkeley.

On the other hand, I never met Payam—at least not that I remember. He was executed in Iran while I was still a child. I've seen one picture of him, taken around the time they started the Berkeley study group. In the photo, he was wearing dark-rimmed glasses and a fatigue-green jacket. His face was turned away from the camera toward the person he was speaking with. Payam was a man who wanted to be the ideal revolutionary.

While Sharam had a family and many friends, Payam had his studies, theories, and comrades. I'm told he never had a girlfriend. He believed in purity of purpose and not owning things, like blenders, pets, or televisions. But he was an artist. When he was alone, he sketched people's faces and their bodies; perhaps this was his way of connecting with others and still keeping his distance.

Sharam and Payam spent hours together, walking around Berkeley, talking and debating everything from imperialism to government corruption to their obligation to the workers of the world versus the workers of Iran.

What should we do about the shah? they often asked.

At that time, across the United States, the anti-war movement was starting to transition from mindful civil actions to militant disobedience. It was the dawning of the age of the radical: Every day news came of another country, somewhere in the world, shrugging off the yoke of imperialism. Revolution was everywhere, and the thinking was it was just a matter of time before it came to the United States and Iran.

Payam and Sharam asked themselves: Should they try to remove the monarch by planning a coup? Or would assassination be more efficient? And what movement should they try to emulate? What movements could they learn from? Were they building their own ideology, brick by brick? Or were they amplifying the ideas of others?

They got lost in these questions. Sitting in their living room, they smoked hundreds of cigarettes as they discussed Marx and Trotsky. One afternoon, while meeting with three of their friends under the leafy canopy of Tilden Park, they decided they wanted to do more than just sit around and talk ideas. They decided to form an organization founded on Marxist-Leninist-Trotskyist theories. The new group called themselves the Organization of Revolutionary Communists.

The young men of the new ORC were in their middle twenties and besotted with the promise and romance of revolution. With time, their organization would evolve past the theories of Marx, Lenin, and Trotsky to include elements of Maoism and Stalinism. Like New Leftists around the world, they adopted a veritable alphabet soup of political theories.

One day, Sharam was picking over the stacks at the university library when he found a book on the history of the Sarbedars, a small fourteenth-century Persian republic that started as a rebellion against the ruling classes.

The leaders of the Sarbedars had been young, like the men of the new ORC, and their state was born out of a revolt that formed as a violent uprising in the jungles of northern Iran.

The Sarbedars' leaders—dervishes, Shiites, and Sunnis—reflected some of the diversity of the region. Their motto roughly translates to, "We will struggle against the inequalities imposed by the tyrants with the help of God, or else give up our *heads on the gallows*." *Sar-be-dar* literally means *head to the gallows*. This was a declaration that they'd die before they'd lose their independence. They intended to build a republic, but in practice, their land functioned like a violent oligarchy. The small republic was short-lived and fractured, and eventually it was pulled back under the control of the Persian empire.

Still, for Payam at least, the Sarbedars were the only true populist uprising in Iran's history. Their story captured his imagination.

~

By the summer of 1970, a year after the ORC formed, another group called the Revolutionary Communists was making its presence felt among those who gathered at the Iran House. The RC not only had a similar name and believed, more or less, the same things as the ORC, but they were more: *more* radical, *more* militant, *more* disciplined.

While practically everyone in Iran House agreed the Iranian monarchy was corrupt and the United States had no place in Iran, and all said that they wanted a government for Iran that allowed the people a say in how they were governed, groups disagreed on how to reach these goals. The RC wanted to be more like the Black Panthers, which were selling Mao's *Little Red Book* at the gates of Berkeley's campus for a dollar each to raise money for their stockpile of weapons. The Panthers said they couldn't sell the books fast enough and got the arms they wanted.

The ORC, the group started by Payam, tried several tacks to build their membership. They sent people to live in Iran so they could send back news from the homeland and establish a following there. They also drove to the Midwest and Southwest to visit campuses and ask students to join their local Iranian Student Association. Once the kids came to the ISA, the thinking was, the clandestine groups could bring those who were the most promising into the fold. The ORC members weren't the only ones being recruited this way. Most of the groups were using the same methods even as they tried to form alliances with underground groups in Iran and around the Middle East and North Africa. Every cadre was jockeying for members, and all were recruiting from the same pool of students.

Payam and Sharam were among those driving from campus to campus. Their perfect recruit was someone highly intellectual, passionate, and willing to act. They wanted people who understood this wasn't a game or a school club. *This* was life-and-death. *This* was about Iran's future.

My father joined the ORC a few years after it formed, and soon he was sent on these college tours to visit ISA chapters and Iran House gatherings. He was even sent to live near cities like Houston and Chicago to recruit promising members. Over the next twelve years, my father was responsible for convincing dozens and dozens of people to join both the ISA and the ORC.

~

Throughout the 1960s, Iranians had been coming to attend American colleges and universities at an extraordinary rate. In the middle 1950s, there were only a few hundred but by 1979, there were just over fifty-one thousand Iranian students studying across the United States—at the time, it was by far the largest group of foreign students studying in the States. In Iran, there was a sort of cachet connected with being able to send a child to the United States for school. It didn't really matter what school. A student visa came easily if a family could pay for it. It was a way of showing off a family's wealth and clout.

These students came to the United States in waves, their arrivals often attached to the school calendar. But the kids weren't clueless. They understood America was a capitalist superpower that stood for some freedom for certain people. They had grown up reading American newspapers, so they followed the civil rights movement and the Vietnam War from afar. Long before they set foot on American soil, they had opinions about the country.

And of course, they were influenced by those who'd come to study before them. It was like a step system: An older sibling or cousin would attend a school first, and then, one by one, their younger relatives would follow. This was how it was for my father. He settled in Berkeley and a few years later his younger brother, my Amu, and his younger sister, my Ameh, came, too.

A couple of years may seem like nothing now but *then*? Three years meant the difference between the Beatles singing about holding hands and letting go; it was the difference between draft numbers being called and draft cards being burned; it was the difference between Nixon's reelection and his resignation, and it was the difference between an oil surplus and a crisis.

Whereas it took my father years to become politicized, it took his siblings no time at all. They landed and were enveloped by the ISA and everything that meant. They were like all Iranian students in the States; they'd grown up watching the close post-1953 relationship between Iran and America. They saw how fast the royal family's wealth was growing and witnessed the power SAVAK had to contain dissent. Their nation no longer had political parties; those who opposed the shah landed in prison. Whether or not they loved their monarch didn't matter: the shah expected and demanded complete loyalty from his subjects. Only a few of the elite had any real say in how the country was governed. Those who criticized the throne risked arrest, prison, torture, or exile.

And then, let's consider where and when these Iranian students landed: By 1970, there were general strikes and violent protests. Professors joined their students for demonstrations, and then back in their classrooms, they dissected what they'd just experienced. These Iranians, many of whom were being supported financially, in part or wholly by their families, now had freedom to take risks, and they had the luxury of time to absorb the lessons of various social movements. Many embraced the American anti-war movement and the anti-war movement embraced them in return.

SIX

Berkeley, California, 1970

R evolution," wrote Chairman Mao in his *Little Red Book*, "is not a dinner party, or writing an essay, or painting a picture, or doing embroidery; it cannot be so refined, so leisurely and gentle, so temperate, kind, courteous, restrained and magnanimous. A revolution is an insurrection, an act of violence by which one class overthrows another."

This was how my parents saw the world then: "One class overthrows another."

This felt to them like the way forward. My parents and their friends weren't going to demonstration after demonstration, one protest or strike after another, simply to demand reformation. They wanted to smash the reset button and trigger a complete overhaul of institutions and power structures. The systems were rotten, and rot must be cut out and discarded.

There was no room for distraction, nothing but their revolutionary mission could matter. The students in these groups dressed similarly to Chinese revolutionaries, their clothing almost like uniforms. The leaders of the various political factions discouraged romantic entanglements to the point of their being outlawed; nonrevolutionary music and scripted television were verboten. Alcohol was given up. Money was communal.

Distractions, as Mao said, must be eschewed until the revolution was realized.

Everything had to be about the movement: Down with the shah. Down with American imperialism. *Death to both!*

The leaders of the many underground political cadres might have been able to convince their followers to forgo booze and drugs, but try to stop love, sex, and romance among those who feel the pull of passion and purpose. What is more alluring than trying to save the world with a beautiful person? What is sexier than working together toward something bigger than oneself?

Since nearly all the leaders were entangled in their own affairs, the hypocrisy bred resentment and forced unnecessary secrets into the Confederation.

~

My mother and Naz were talking one morning, when my mother invited her to come on a day trip to Monterey. My father was waiting outside of the apartment to drive them. He was in his midtwenties, one of the older members at the Iran House. Naz was nineteen and while she was a member of the Iranian Student Association and Iran House, she wasn't part of those secretive political factions. She'd barely ever spoken to my father. Her older sister, Roya, was a member of the Revolutionary Communists, though Naz didn't know that then.

The three drove down the coast and after a couple of hours, they decided to stop and explore the beach. They wandered aimlessly, looking into the tide pools along the shoreline. The beach wasn't covered with sand but with sea glass, smooth pebbles, and minuscule shells, and it was nearly deserted, as if the day and the beach were theirs alone.

None of them talked about anything particularly important. My mother and Naz talked about their classes, and my father told them about his work as a senior design engineer with the Signetics Corporation in Sunnyvale. At that time, he was working and going to school, and every penny of his $17,000 a year went to supporting the ORC and its members. None of them mentioned politics or whatever political activities they had planned for the summer. Naz didn't know that my mother was deciding between the two organizations, the Organization of Revolutionary Communists and the Revolutionary Communists. Naz didn't know about these tensions. Yet, here they were, wasting a day as if they hadn't a care in the world. As if nothing else mattered at all.

Much later, Naz thought that perhaps this day marked my parents' beginning. Maybe they'd wanted to spend time together but didn't want to raise suspicion, so they invited her to come along. Everyone says that's how it was then: people held on to so many secrets that seemed important but don't matter at all anymore. Unnecessary secrets hurt people and foment division, even when that secret is just two people falling in love.

Bijan found out about my parents months after the summer they'd begun, and after he found out, he was furious. They'd lied. They'd lied to *him*. They'd used his friendship as their cover when they met in the small room Bijan rented as a political meeting place for people to talk without fear of being overheard. One day, Bijan had gone to the room looking for my father, and my mother opened the door half-dressed, expecting my father. Bijan never forgave them, or at least he never forgave my mother. They were supposed to be his closest friends and they hadn't told him anything about it.

~

On Friday morning, June 26, Naz was getting ready in her new apartment, one she shared with her older sister. She didn't realize her move had signaled a shift in political allegiances. Everyone thought she'd joined her sister's group, the Revolutionary Communists, but she hadn't. Naz wasn't privy to the internal machinations occurring just under the surface at the Iran House. Still, she felt the tension: people who had been best friends weren't speaking anymore; they barely looked at each other, and these breakups were happening quickly.

That morning, she had stepped out of the shower and wrapped a towel around herself as she walked into her bedroom when the telephone rang. She lifted the handset to her ear. She was told to grab her camera and come downstairs, where a couple of rented vans and forty Iranians, many of them her closest friends, were waiting. Among them were six women, including her sister, Roya. Naz was the youngest and perhaps the least politically active of the women there.

She was, as far as I can tell, the final recruit for the mission. A petite, bubbly young woman with a wide smile, she always took pictures of everything: Roommates and friends staying up all night laughing and talking, sitting cross-legged on the floor and smoking. Friends mugging and posing as they bunched close to each other outside. Sometimes her camera caught them unaware with their mouths open as they talked over one another. She was, for a time, the closest thing the Iranian Student Association and the Iran House had to an official photographer.

That Friday morning her friends said they needed her to come along and take pictures, so she pulled on a pair of jeans and a T-shirt and slipped on shoes. She slung her camera's strap over her shoulder like a purse, and as she ran down the stairs of the building, it swung cheerfully back and forth as if she were going to a party.

She wouldn't have gone if she had known what she would be doing. She would have begged off had she known she'd spend thirty-five days in jail and wouldn't be able to get her Iranian passport renewed. She wouldn't have gone if she had known her name would be printed in Iran's newspapers and her family would be questioned. If she'd known that she wouldn't be able to go back home, she would have finished getting ready and ignored the call. She might not have felt angry and betrayed, and her resentment wouldn't have lingered for decades.

~

For weeks, leaders of three political factions—the National Front, the Revolutionary Communists, and the Organization of Revolutionary Communists—working under the auspices of the Confederation—had been fighting, arguing, haranguing, and negotiating, trying to agree on how to take over the Iranian consulate in San Francisco. A takeover meant arrests, so there had to be a team that would stay behind and handle whatever fallout there was.

My father's job during the takeover was to work the phones: he'd call lawyers and organize bail. He couldn't risk getting arrested, because it would put his Signetics job at risk, and at that time, the ORC relied on his money.

My mother hadn't originally been planning to stay in Berkeley for the summer. Her father sent her a plane ticket to come visit him in Iran, but the political leaders of these three groups didn't approve. They convinced her to stay, reminding her that they all had an obligation to the cause.

So, she agreed to be the heart of their communications team, assigned to work with the press on the day of the consulate takeover and in the days that followed.

The takeover was planned as a response to the announcement that Princess Ashraf Pahlavi, the shah's twin sister, would represent Iran at the twenty-fifth anniversary session of the United Nations. The news shouldn't have surprised anyone. By 1970, Ashraf Pahlavi had already spent seven years as a delegate to the UN, including a year as the chair of the UN Commission on Human Rights, one of the highest-profile appointments at the international organization. She was only the second woman, after Eleanor Roosevelt, to hold the position. Still, the announcement infuriated many anti-shah activists who felt the princess personified the worst excesses of the Iranian monarchy.

Princess Ashraf didn't particularly care for the activists either. She was fifty years old and an ardent feminist who steadfastly supported women's equality around the world, but she was anything but a radical.

At some other time in history perhaps, her work in women's and human rights would have been a source of great national pride—for many it was and is. But for the anti-shah activists, the princess was synonymous with corruption and American imperialism, so every move she made and every sentence she uttered were seen through this filter.

The syndicated feature called "The Lighter Side of Washington," by the columnist Betty Beale, beautifully captured the paradox of the princess's public image. At a glittering Washington fete held in her honor at the Iranian Embassy, Princess Ashraf was described as "slim, chic, brainy." But, Beale wrote, the princess "looked like no feminist you ever ran into. She was wearing a crown of diamonds and pink rubies that matched her three-tiered diamond-ruby necklace above a pink crystal and pearl covered Dior gown."

The princess knew that many young Iranians, especially those living in the West, were passionately against the Pahlavi government. They believed that the shah was perpetrating human rights abuses even as she was making her name as a human rights crusader. The king projected an increasingly lavish public persona and she was seen as an extension of her brother. She buoyed his image and championed his reforms, even as she tried to create some space between her work and his government.

The activists on the political left who were foisting placards knew that Iranians were being denied a political voice, tossed into prison for speaking out, and stalked by SAVAK agents abroad. At the opposite end of the spectrum, Islamists in Iran—and their leader Ayatollah Khomeini, a Shiite religious leader who wielded influence from exile—saw the princess's image and the women's rights movement as examples of the corrupting influence of Western imperialism. They saw the princess and her work as an affront to tradition and religion.

None of this was happening in a vacuum—the United States was in chaos by 1970. On April 28, President Richard Nixon authorized sending ground forces into Cambodia, a country the United States had been bombing for more than a year. In response, a general strike started on May 1 and gained steam after National Guard troops shot and killed four students at Kent State University on May 4. Hundreds more high schools, colleges, and universities joined the strike in the days that followed, and on May 9, the day after Nixon held a press conference justifying his Cambodian Incursion, one hundred thousand people marched on Washington, DC. Six days later, city and state police fired hundreds of rounds of ammunition at strikers at a demonstration at the majority Black Jackson State College in Jackson, Mississippi, killing two people. More deaths and violence followed: Six students were killed and at least sixty-two wounded in Augusta, Georgia. Eleven students were bayoneted and arrested at the University of New Mexico. By the end of May thousands of activists had been arrested and more than one hundred people had been killed or injured by National Guard troops or law enforcement.

Nearly half of the country's eight million students and three hundred fifty thousand faculty participated in the strike. The crisis spurred a growing radicalization and militantness that had already started. In February, students in the small college town of Isla Vista, California, burned the Bank of America building to the ground—the first of many arson and bombing incidents in the United States that year. Reserve Officers' Training Corps (ROTC) centers were set on fire or bombed. Explosions went off on campuses and in buildings across the country. In 1971 and 1972, there were about two thousand five hundred domestic bombings.

Into this maelstrom came news from Iran that there was a crackdown on political dissidents, and many of those arrested had been working with the student movement abroad. As news of the arrests reached the Iranian activists in the United States, the leaders of the Iranian Student Association in Berkeley decided it was time to take action against the Pahlavi regime.

The princess's appointment, the arrests of political dissidents inside Iran, and the general fervor of the 1970 May crisis all served as the backdrop as a plan for forty-one people to take over the Iranian consulate started to take shape.

~

In order to make sure that news of the impending takeover didn't leak out to the consulate staff—or worse, to an undercover SAVAK agent at one of the various Northern California universities—its organizers kept the specifics of the plan secret. Whenever it came time to take a particular action, they handpicked a group of trusted people to participate.

On the morning of the takeover, a young couple walked into the consulate to ask how they could get married as Iranians living in the United States. As they listened to the answers, they also counted the employees working in the office and noted the number of doors that led in and out of the building.

As the people in the vans waited for a signal, Naz realized that the demonstration she thought she'd signed up for was in fact something entirely different. The group got out of the vans and walked into the building, adrenaline flooding their bodies. They pushed past the staff into one room and then in another room they scrawled anti-shah slogans across the walls. Someone painted "Down with U.S. Imperialism" in large letters. Naz moved stiffly, frozen at the edge of a formal dining room. She watched two of her friends dip brushes into red paint they must have brought with them and write "Death to the Shah" across the stark white tablecloths.

Naz thought of her mother, who had always taken great care to wash and iron her white linens, which were identical to the ones her friends were destroying. Then, she heard the voices around her start to rise.

The staff were shouting and her friends sneered; Naz tried to find someplace she could hide. She slipped inside the kitchen, where the cook, his wife, and one of the activists were waiting for the thing to end. They stayed put until the police came.

While people were shoving their way through the building, one protester, who had helped plan the takeover, planted himself by the front door of the consulate to make sure everyone got in. He yelled at his comrades to stay out of the upstairs area, where the consul and his family lived. The plan was to bring the press inside the consulate, but the police got there first and set up a perimeter around the property. The protesters tried to negotiate with the police, but the cops rushed the door and pressed the protesters against a wall, hitting them over and over again.

All at once and altogether, everyone seemed to lose their minds. The activists pulled pictures of the royal family off the wall and smashed them against the furniture. Tchotchkes shattered on the ground. Officers dragged the forty-one activists from the consulate, loaded them into a police van, and carted them off to the city jail.

~

Sharam remembers that he was the first person the group was able to bail out. He said he contacted the lawyer Terence Hallinan for advice. Hallinan would later become district attorney for San Francisco. The police had confiscated the vans, and when they searched them, they found a notebook filled with detailed notes from the planning. The notebook gave the prosecution a case for conspiracy and they tacked on a kidnapping charge, too.

There was no way for the forty-one to get out of having to serve some time, Hallinan told him.

But remember, most of the people who participated in the takeover weren't involved in the planning. Many of them hadn't realized the price of participation would be so steep.

Within days of the protesters' arrest in San Francisco, authorities in Iran brought in their family members for questioning. Iranian newspapers printed the first name, last name, and political affiliation of every person involved or suspected of being involved in the takeover. The list included not only those who participated that morning, but those like my parents who'd worked to support the takeover.

The Iranian government asked the United States to send these students back to Iran to be dealt with there. But the United States refused, so the shah's government refused to renew the passports of those involved in planning or implementing the event that became known as the *Chello-Yek Nafar*, the Forty-One People. The shah pushed through a law that any person affiliated with the Confederation of Iranian Students who returned to Iran would be subject to prosecution. With that, every member of the Confederation, all over the world and regardless of their level of activism, was effectively exiled.

~

Back in San Francisco, lawyers were eventually able to plead down the kidnapping charges. The court documents state that the activists were charged with "invading and damaging the premises of the Iranian consulate and holding the occupants hostage under threat of death." On advice of counsel, the forty-one activists pleaded guilty to charges of false imprisonment and served thirty-five days in the city jail. Newspapers in the United States printed a picture of police dragging one man down the steps of the consulate.

Those members who'd thought the anti-shah movement was a lark, a way to hang out with other Iranians and talk about politics, now found themselves unable to return home. They were angry and felt deeply betrayed by the leaders they had looked to for guidance. They believed, and some still believe, that those who planned the *Chello-Yek Nafar* knew the risks and purposely didn't tell them what might happen to them. Many left the movement and some, like Naz, left Berkeley altogether. She might not have been able to go back to Iran, but she figured she could at least get on with her life.

Others, like my parents, had an entirely different reaction. Now that they couldn't go back to Iran, they felt that they had nothing to lose. The shah could forbid political speech and action in Iran, but he had no jurisdiction in California. SAVAK agents could try and infiltrate the Confederation and Iran House, the FBI could start files and approach members of the organization, but it didn't change the mission. Their mission was to disseminate information against the shah and his government, and encourage a revolution. They figured it would take decades, but those who remained after the *Chello-Yek Nafar* were more passionately committed than before.

One would think that the fallout from the takeover would bring together the disparate political groups, but instead it only highlighted the animosity between them. That summer, while many of the *Chello-Yek Nafar* sat in jail, arguments between the interim leaders of the Organization of Revolutionary Communists and the Revolutionary Communists, National Front sympathizers, and unaffiliated members of Iran House became hostile. Alliances were formed and broken, while infighting and backstabbing became the norm.

~

My mother and my father worked together every day that summer after the *Chello-Yek Nafar*. It was their responsibility to make sure the press stayed interested and the lawyers were paid.

On warm days, my mother joined other friends at my father's apartment, where the smell of chlorine from a pool permeated the whole building. At least that's what my father's baby sister, Ameh, remembers most about his apartment. She was nine and was visiting California with her parents. She'd never met her brother, Faramarz, before then. That summer, she was the unofficial Iran House mascot, and my father's girlfriend, Joy, took care of her in all the small ways children remember. One time when Ameh was hungry, Joy took two pieces of white bread, buttered them, and melted orange American cheese in between; then she slid the sandwich onto a plate, cut it into triangles, and handed it to the girl. The American grilled cheese, a delicacy with a faintly chemical flavor, was the most delicious, the most decadent meal Ameh had ever had. She took one bite and nearly died of happiness.

Some floors below, my father was with his friends, talking around the pool. My mother was also there, sitting so her tan legs dangled in the water. She was talking and joking, calling out to one friend or another.

When my parents were near each other, they didn't touch.

But Joy remembers that all at once my mother was around. All at once, it seemed as if she was everywhere.

~

Joy had met my father years earlier, in 1967, at a ballroom dancing class. She had long, straight strawberry-blond hair and had gone to a Catholic high school in San Rafael. My father had a calm self-assuredness, a nice smile, and a soft, unplaceable accent. He walked up to her and asked her to dance. She took his hand and they tried to follow the instructor's commands. She noticed that he didn't move like the other boys.

This is something different, she thought.

That's when their four-year love affair began. It changed her as love does, whether big or small. Love always changes us. It gave her direction. It set a path for a time. Their first summer together was also the Summer of Love, which was misnamed, as it spanned nearly the whole year. It began that January at a protest concert where the poet Allen Ginsberg blew on a conch shell, and it carried on through the release of the Scott McKenzie single "San Francisco (Be Sure to Wear Some Flowers in Your Hair)," which was at least partially responsible for encouraging more than seventy-five thousand young people from across the country to descend on the Haight-Ashbury neighborhood. It was as if the Bay Area were suddenly a magnet and people were pulled into there from everywhere. The Summer of Love ended in the fall when the Haight's frustrated denizens held a ceremony called the "Death of the Hippie" to kick the new kids out of their city.

When Joy and my father met, this was all noise, like the rocking, wailing San Francisco sound heard from the open doors and car windows all around them. They were box stepping and foxtrotting. They went for long walks, shared meals, and dropped in on demonstrations. My father told her about his family and took her to Tuesday nights at Iran House. She met his friends. He took her back to his apartment, where he, Bijan, and Bijan's older brother perfected the art of making Persian rice with a crispy bottom crust that was nearly as good as their mothers'.

They spent weekends together camping in Yosemite and hiked the trails for hours. He made her laugh; he made her angry. He was finding his place and so was she. My father wasn't particularly good at writing to his family in Iran, so Joy took over his correspondence. She wrote letters to Ameh. She sent the girl a green nightgown and a matching robe.

Joy wasn't politically dogmatic; she was liberal and for a brief time, an active member of the leftist groups Students for a Democratic Society and the Radical Student Union. My father introduced her to the ISA. She eventually moved in with several of the Iran House cohort. She, like Naz, took pictures at all the demonstrations and events. She wasn't the only American woman involved. There were several. As the ISA began to house a political movement, more young American women joined; many, though not all, were dating Iranian men.

Like all couples, Joy and my father fought. After one blowup, she went to his apartment so they could talk. Soon the anger faded, he apologized, and they laughed about whatever it was that had made them so angry.

It's easy to say sorry, my father told her, half teasing, *because I know I'm right.*

For years, whenever Joy found herself choking on an apology, an "I'm sorry" she was saying because she wanted peace and to move on, she remembered my father's line and smiled.

But later, I wondered about this. When a person was forced to concede and apologize about something critical, when they believed they were right, wouldn't resentment settle like an anvil on their chest? Wouldn't the anger grow until it felt like it was breaking their ribs?

∼

Within a year of *Chello-Yek Nafar*, the Northern California chapter of the Iranian Student Association had transformed completely. Now it was a loose coalition of political factions hampered by sectarianism and shifting alliances. With every fissure the groups changed names, until the organization became a complicated maze of allegiances and betrayals.

As I tried to unknot these threads—the monarchists from the nationalists from the leftists from the Islamists, the younger from the older, the rich from the poor, the children of merchants from those of the civil servants, and on and on—I felt myself grow angrier and more frustrated until, finally, I deflated.

This was, my mother later said, the beginning of the end for the ISA. In a 1991 interview with her sister[8] for my aunt's book *Women in Exile*, my mother tried very hard to explain the roots of the Confederation's political sectarianism. She was still sorting through the detritus of grief, trauma, pain, and guilt. Her stories jumped around. She doubled back through time. She repeated herself. Her tone stayed controlled, as if she were removed from the stories of her own life. She laid a great deal of blame on the Revolutionary Communists, the more militant group that competed for power against the Organization of Revolutionary Communists. She credited them with pushing the militancy and radicalism that swept the Confederation in the 1970s.

---

8   My mother gave several interviews about her time in the Confederation, including two that were conducted by her sister. One is an oral history of my mother's time with the movement, and the other is a more intimate account of my mother's life, which was adapted as a chapter for the book *Women in Exile*, published by the University of Virginia in 1994. I draw from both.

"They split the movement into one thousand parts," my mother said. "They destroyed its vitality. Within one year, they destroyed the organization."

~

I will go back to Iran, my father told Joy one day after they'd been dating for a couple of years. *I will go back. One day, I will go.*

I'll come with you, she said.

No, he said.

But why? Joy asked. *Why? Why can't I come with? Why can't we go together?*

No, he said, his tone firm. *My life in Iran will be and can* only *be about this. I'll go underground. Do you understand? I won't exist.*

Joy watched him as he spoke. His eyes were clear green. His jaw clenched. His broad shoulders set in a straight line. He spoke as if he saw the future clearly, as if he and he alone knew what would be. In this future, there was only revolution. He was called to it. It was fated.

I don't understand, she said, though she did, and she didn't.

I don't understand, she said, again.

But Joy understood enough. She understood he was saying that he wasn't hers. She loved him and he was telling her he would leave one day.

And yet. And *yet.*

She loved him.

~

Joy told me the outlines of this conversation nearly fifty years later.

"If he knew this was what was going to happen," I asked, my voice shaking, "why did he decide to have a family?"

Her eyes were so kind and filled with such sympathy I had to look away.

~

Washington, DC, 2014

Time slipped the longer I picked at the past. I moved in and out of the present; sometimes I could effortlessly hold the two realities, now and then, at once and without issue.

Other times, it was as if I had misplaced myself. As if I were a time traveler and the present didn't belong to me, nor, for that matter, did the past. I came to feel I was living out of time. Like I was loving out of time. As if I were out of time and living apart from a timeline.

I ran into my mother everywhere. She rose like an apparition from yellowing pages lying in the middle of a forgotten box. I found her in photo albums I thought we'd lost. I found her always at times when I didn't expect to.

One night, I was at my kitchen counter with my laptop open, wasting time wandering down the twists and turns of the internet, when I found a link to an old news clip on the Bay Area Television Archive. The description read as follows:

> KQED News report from October 15th, 1971 in San Francisco featuring scenes from a large demonstration by Iranians, protesting against the Shah of Iran and his regime's celebration of the 2500th anniversary of the Persian Empire. Includes views of angry protestors [sic] marching, making speeches and an interview with a woman, who feels that Iran should

be funding basic social welfare programs rather than expensive celebrations.[9]

"An interview with a woman." A woman who could have been anyone. I pressed the triangle on the black-and-white thumbnail, and the footage began to roll. It opened on demonstrators gathering by a rectangular fountain. The sun's glare was bouncing off the reflective surfaces and glass accents of the office building. The wind blew so strongly the water in the fountain splashed the passersby.

Protesters were dressed like Maoist revolutionaries in loose-fitting fatigues and low-brimmed hats that obscured their facial features. Some wore black armbands, a gesture of solidarity with the Cambodians and Vietnamese killed by the US military. They dressed alike and hid their faces because they didn't want to be recognized. If the news cameras showed their faces on the evening news, they'd be marked as part of the anti-shah movement, they wouldn't be able to renew their passports or return to Iran, and the safety of their families back in Iran would be jeopardized.

The anti-shah activists knew they were being watched and monitored by two governments: the United States and Iran. The FBI had been infiltrating anti-war and leftist groups by dispatching plainclothes agents to attend rallies as news photographers or as participants. These agents would then be recruited and sent to colleges to join campus groups, where they would report on members and their activities.

The shah's secret security force, the SAVAK, was trained by the CIA and was joining the ISA, going to the Iran House events, and generally trying to integrate into campus life. SAVAK also hired people to attend

---

9   KQED. "Iranian Demonstration in San Francisco." News report from October 15, 1971, in San Francisco, California. https://diva.sfsu.edu/collections/sfbatv/bundles/189745

anti-shah rallies and cause trouble for the protesters—they might start a fight or disturbance or simply shout pro-shah slogans.

But in this footage the Iranian activists must have only started to become paranoid; their masks covered only part of their faces. By the next year, their faces would be completely obscured except for small openings for the eyes, nose, and mouth. These activists, like their American brethren, came by their paranoia honestly. All of them may not have been under surveillance, but some were. Some being watched was enough to stoke fear in all.

As the film played on my computer, the camera panned over posters and placards. The audio squeaked and recalibrated.

Then, I heard my mother's disembodied voice.

A half sentence, before the sound was cut. For a second, I thought I'd imagined it.

But then, there she was on my screen, her arms crossed, as she walked around the perimeter of the demonstration.

The audio and the images were, at times, out of step. It was as if someone taped together scraps found on a newsroom floor. I watched, hoping Mom would reappear, and she did. This time she looked straight at the camera—straight at me—through dark sunglasses and from under a low-brimmed cap across the decades.

She's so young, I thought. *So young that she doesn't quite know how to hold herself, yet. Her mannerisms are being tried on still. They're just shadows of the ones I'd come to know so well.*

"There are demonstrations in Washington and San Francisco today, in order to expose the celebrations that are taking place in Iran, and expose the nature of the regime in Iran, which is a fascistic, tyrannical, repressive regime in Iran," she said to the camera. "We're trying to expose the reality, the contradiction between what the regime states about the nature of the celebrations and, in reality, what they are."

The celebration she was talking about was the twenty-five-hundred-year anniversary of Iran's monarchy, which was held in a lavish tent city thousands of miles away, in the desert near Persepolis. It was an event that was covered by all the major news outlets. Here's part of the *New York Times* report from the weekend:

> The Shah of Iran established himself tonight as one of the world's greatest party givers. For sheer grandeur, his gala in a silk tent will be hard for any nation to surpass.

The *Times* goes on to describe the feast catered by Maxim's de Paris with "partridge with foie gras and truffle stuffing and wines ranging from a pink Dom Pérignon to a Château Lafite from the Rothschild vineyard."

For six months, the Iranian Air Force had sent "sorties between Shiraz and Paris flying goods which were then trucked carefully in army lorries to Persepolis." The event featured air-conditioned tents, Italian drapes and curtains, Baccarat crystal, Limoges china with the Pahlavi coat of arms, and five thousand bottles of wine. Hundreds of horses and nearly two thousand soldiers marched in the opening parade. There was a film commissioned called "Flame of Persia," narrated by Orson Welles. The Versailles florist Georges Truffaut created a rose and cypress garden in the middle of the great tent city.

It was arguably the most extravagant state function in modern history. The press reported that the festivities cost the Iranian government close to $100 million, though the Iranian government later claimed the affair totaled just $16 million. In the days leading up to the celebration, details of the party had begun to leak to the press.

My mother, demonstrating a world away in California, said to the camera: "This money is coming from the people in Iran, a people whose average worker earns less than a dollar a day, which is one-sixth of his needs for his expenses; a country who still has eight-five percent illiteracy; a country whose children still suffer, thirty percent, from malnutrition—"

Again, she was cut off; the camera showed the crowd. I looked for my father. He might have been somewhere, tucked in a corner of the frame, but I didn't know him like I knew my mother. I had her voice, her walk, and her face memorized.

~

The film was a strange, cobbled thing. It cut between marchers, police barricades, and the rally at the federal building. It showed my mother close-up—a tight shot of her face and then a frame of her lips. But interspersed with these shots were clips of a blown-apart building and men in hard hats walking over piles of busted drywall and refuse. A man was sitting in a truck embossed with the logo of a local glass company, looking into the camera lens and smiling.

The cameraman asked him to get out of the truck.

"Certainly," the man said. He opened the door and disappeared.

There was broken glass on the pavement and then a close-up of a mannequin dressed as the shah. It was an effigy lashed to a truck decorated with signs that called for the end of the monarchy and the shah's death. Images of protesters punching their fists into the air were spliced throughout.

The images were like a dream sequence in a Luis Buñuel film. Sitting at my kitchen counter in 2014, staring into 1971, I was confused and disoriented. The exploded building was the Iranian consulate in San Francisco, bombed the night before the demonstration at which my mother was speaking.

Were these two events related? Could my parents have been involved in the bombing?

If they were, did that change who they were to me?

Did that change everything or precisely nothing at all?

~

In September 1971, a month before the explosion and the protest, there was a prison uprising in Attica, New York. One of the leaders of the riots was a man named Sam Melville, an activist responsible for bombing eight government and commercial buildings in Manhattan in 1969. Before his incarceration, Melville was known as the Johnny Appleseed of guerrilla bombings because he taught political militants how to build bombs triggered by timers. He was killed in the Attica uprising.

In October, a month after his death and the night before the demonstration where my mother spoke on camera, the Iranian consulate was bombed. The Iranian consul blamed the Iranian students. The students denied any involvement.

Four days later, several media outlets received letters from a group that called itself the Sam Melville Squadron of the Revolutionary Army. The group, which wasn't affiliated with the Iranian Student Association, the Organization of Revolutionary Communists, or even the transnational Confederation of Iranian Students, claimed responsibility for the bombing as retaliation for the Attica riots. The letters dedicated the bombing "to all the prisoners in the torture camps of the Warden Shah of Iran."

This was another example of the close links between American and Iranian groups—an act of violence in solidarity with the Attica prisoners perpetrated against the Iranian consulate, in solidarity with the anti-shah movement.

I was relieved that my parents had nothing to do with the bombing—at least as far as I could tell. For a brief time, though, I wasn't sure. This uncertainty unsettled me. It challenged me. I was relieved because now the uncertainty was past.

I no longer needed to wonder how their involvement would've changed my view of them. I was relieved because finding an answer to that particular question didn't matter anymore.

~

It was two weeks after this demonstration that the leaders of the Organization of Revolutionary Communists asked my parents to get married. This way my father would have a clear path to a green card and could spend more time organizing and recruiting. The leadership didn't know my parents were having an affair. On October 21, 1971, my parents drove to Reno. After a brief ceremony, someone at the courthouse handed my mother a homemaker's kit: a bag filled with an assortment of detergents and an apron to help her keep house.

When I asked my mother about their wedding, she said that it wasn't a romantic story. She said that they took a half day off work and she got a bag of soap. We both laughed.

~

After my parents married, my father continued to visit Joy, who was, by then, living and going to school in San Francisco. She noticed that he'd grown colder, and his visits were farther apart. One night at the Iran House—or maybe it was someplace else, but it was probably there—Joy, my mother, and my father were together in a crowd of friends.

They were, each of them, a point of a triangle; they could feel the other points shifting and contracting. Joy could feel that something had changed. Was it that my mother and father had grown closer? My mother probably felt that there was something unfinished between my father and Joy. All that contraction, the pushing and pulling together and apart, jostled the three.

I thought it was over between you and Faramarz, my mother said to Joy.

When I heard this story later, I could see my mother's face so clearly: her lips pressing together into a thin line, her shoulders squared, and her jaw locked.

She could put up with a lot—the secrecy and the green-card marriage—but she was done being part of this. She had not agreed to this. She was done hurting this woman, and she was done being hurt.

She was done.

My mother told my father it was over; my father ended things with Joy, and Joy never heard from either of them again.

When I met Joy, she was living in her family's house, the same place Ameh had described to me, tucked into the San Rafael hills. When she opened the door, she saw me, with my mother's face and my father's eyes, looking back at her. There I was, the answer to all her questions.

"He was the love of my life," she said later that day as we sat across from each other in an empty Thai restaurant.

I felt tender and protective toward this woman who loved my father still and who, all these years later, defended him passionately. No one spoke about my father like this except for my mother when she was alive, and maybe then not even she.

"I'm sorry," I said before I left.

I was apologizing for a hurt I had nothing to do with. I was sorry that Joy had to learn everything from me. That I was the one to look her in the eye and tell her what happened to my father and my mother and her friends. I came from nowhere with a message of how they had gone on after her and how they had ended.

As I drove away from her house, down the Pacific Coast highway toward Monterey, the late afternoon light made the rolling hills glow gold. In one visit, dark corners of this story were illuminated.

SEVEN

Iran and Iraq, 1970

On June 21, 1970, two students from the University of Tehran and a twelve-year-old boy boarded an Iran National Airlines Boeing 727 leaving Tehran for Kuwait. Thirty minutes after takeoff, they walked into the first-class cabin toward the cockpit carrying bottles filled with gasoline. They let the petrol pour along the floor, while people smoked cigarettes all around them. The men then pulled out .22-caliber pistols and ordered the pilots to fly them to Iraq. Radio Baghdad reported that when the plane landed, the hijackers asked for asylum—and the Iraqi government granted it.

This was the first hijacking that Iranian students and anti-shah activists carried out that year where they demanded to be flown to the Iraqi capital; there would be another in October. Iran and Iraq were in the midst of a serious territorial dispute over the natural border dividing them. Both nations pulled their diplomats out of the other's country.

The Iraqi government gave the hijackers a job to go with their asylum: broadcasting anti-shah propaganda into Iran via Radio Baghdad. Eventually, over seven years, the Iraqis would give the anti-shah movement at least five radio stations to use against the monarch.

The new radio programmers had relationships not only with the leftist guerrilla movement in Iran, but with the international Iranian student movement generally and, Sharam told me years later, the Organization of Revolutionary Communists specifically. Once their radio program was up and running, it was staffed by a steady influx of young Iranians flown in from Europe, the Middle East, and the United States. More than a year later, and months after guerrilla groups started raising hell in Iran, my father landed in Baghdad to begin working at the station. He was now married to an American citizen and had a green card and a glowing reference from Signetics. He was one of the best recruiters the ORC had; now they could send him anywhere in the world on an assignment and know they could call him back easily.

Giving over a radio station to angry guerrilla fighters wasn't the only way Iraq chose to help an enemy of its enemy. By early 1970, the exiled Shiite religious leader Ayatollah Ruhollah Khomeini had become a powerful opponent of the shah, and he was living in Najaf, Iraq.

The animosity between Khomeini and the shah had started nearly a decade earlier when the monarch introduced a package of legislative reforms dubbed the White Revolution. One reform promised to take land from the wealthy and redistribute it, and another gave women the right to vote.

The landowners were furious and so was Khomeini, who, as a cleric, was among the country's largest landowners. Khomeini worried not only that the new reforms would snatch away his wealth, but that they also signaled a new age of secularism. He became politicized, and from that point on relentlessly and ferociously attacked the monarch from his pulpit. Khomeini saw efforts of modernization as signs of creeping Western imperialism. He preached that the White Revolution was an assault on Islam, tradition, and piety.

The religious students, many of whom were devoted to the radical cleric, began to organize protests against the shah. The shah responded to Khomeini and the protesters with complete disdain, calling them "numb and dispirited snakes and lice who float in their own dirt."

"If these sordid and vile elements with their reactionary friends do not awake from their sleep of ignorance," he said, "the fist of justice, like thunder will . . . terminate their filthy and shameful life."

On March 22, 1963, the shah made good on his promise. Soldiers dressed in plain clothes stormed the Feyzieh, a famous seminary in Qom, a holy town close to Tehran where Khomeini lived. The troops tore through the building, allegedly pushing students off balconies, destroying furniture and literature, and setting fire to piles of turbans and robes.

Several months later, on June 3, 1963, Khomeini gave another angry sermon against the monarch, calling him a "wretched, miserable man." He accused the shah of being Jewish, of being against Islam, and of being against Iran's religious class. He was arrested by SAVAK forces two days later. Once news of his arrest spread, Khomeini's followers and sympathizers descended on the police station in protest.

The police fired into the crowd, killing twenty-eight. In Tehran, two thousand young people congregated at the large, crowded bazaar in southern Tehran. The demonstrations turned into riots and the riots spread across the country. For several days, the protesters, many of whom were religious and secular students, clashed with police before the shah's forces finally were able to get control and quell the unrest.

The end of the 1963 riots effectively stopped organized, open dissent against the shah inside Iran. It was driven underground, and in time, militant guerrilla groups began to emerge. The Iranian student movement outside of the country became the main voice of opposition from 1963 through the 1970s. Eventually the groups inside and those outside the country, in Europe and the United States, were able to connect with each other.

Khomeini spent ten months under house arrest before he was exiled. First he went to Turkey, and then to Iraq, where he was a welcome guest of the government. The Iraqi government gave him a home in the holy city of Najaf, the beating heart of Shiism, where he continued to work and preach against the shah. While the majority of Shiite Muslims live in Iran, Najaf was the home of Imam Ali, the cousin and son-in-law of the Prophet Muhammad, the man who Shiites believe was the prophet's successor. Najaf holds his golden shrine with its shining dome and minarets.

Each year Shiite pilgrims, most from Iran, come to pray at the mosque, multiplying the city's population and providing a direct connection between the two countries. Khomeini stayed in his sparsely furnished home, working on his theories of theology and governance for nearly thirteen years. His students and advisors took his sermons to the public, those who were praying outside his home.

It was here that Khomeini patiently stoked the revolution. In January and February of 1970, he gave a series of sermons that when taken together laid out his plan for a Shiite theocracy. A student took down his words and bound them into a book called *Islamic Government*. The sermons were also recorded onto tapes and smuggled into Iran. Khomeini's message resonated. He was able to tap into growing discontent in Iran, while stoking anti-shah and anti-Western fervor.

It was also from this seat that Khomeini and his advisors first made contact with Iranian student groups in Iran, Europe, and the United States. His clerics traveled north to Baghdad, where they met with Iranian leftists like my father and the others manning the radio station. My father and the others visited Najaf. It is said they got an audience with the ayatollah. They certainly read Khomeini's book and perhaps they helped broadcast his teachings through their radio signal. An alliance was forming between the leftists and Khomeini's followers.

Coalition building was becoming a crucial part of the Organization of Revolutionary Communists' strategy. They sent their members into places like Iraq, Kuwait, Palestine, Yemen, and Saudi Arabia in order to build relationships with groups sympathetic to their cause and to get insurgency training from guerillas working across the Middle East.

Except for the trip to Najaf, my father's time in Iraq was limited to the radio station. He lived at the station, sharing his space with at least one other person. They took turns broadcasting propaganda—a long, long shift that lasted about a month until another person or two would arrive to relieve them.

A radio station runs on a strict schedule, and so did my father. He and his station mate warded off boredom by doing push-ups, sit-ups, and yoga poses. He likely folded in the drills he had learned during the months of required military training he had to complete as an undergrad at Missouri S&T. During the times he wasn't working, he may have run along the path by the Tigris River, which bisects central Baghdad. In the early 1970s, Baghdad was not yet synonymous with Saddam Hussein, smart bombs, and incessant, relentless warring, as it would be decades later. Then, it was a bustling metropolis where the streets were lined with palm trees and clogged by luxury automobiles and red double-decker buses. It was a place of contrasts: colonial European architecture set next to a traditional covered bazaar, while modern round buildings stood out against a bright blue sky.

My father was methodical; he treated his time in Baghdad like a deployment. Nothing else mattered.

Not even my mother ending their relationship before he left California.

~

While my father was in Iraq, my mother was in Yemen.

Yemen had ended an eight-year civil war, and the south had changed its name from the People's Republic of South Yemen to the People's *Democratic* Republic of South Yemen, a sign that the state had taken a sharp turn toward Marxism. It was the only Marxist nation in the Middle East. No one seemed to know exactly where my mother was—Sanaa or Aden or someplace else? No one knew exactly what she was doing there, other than getting "communication training from the guerrillas."

All she later told me about the trip was that she brought home a present for her best friend: a pair of silver earrings, which were intricately rendered discs with a round blue stone set in the middle of each. By the time my mother came back to the United States, the fissures between the groups—the Organization of Revolutionary Communists, the Revolutionary Communists, and the others—had grown so vast that best friends had stopped talking. She never gave the earrings to her friend and she never wore them herself. They stayed in the plastic the shopkeeper had placed them in nearly fifty years ago. That's where they are now, tucked in the file box with Mom's birth certificate and naturalization papers, and all of her grade school and college transcripts. Her time in Yemen is a mystery; what remains, it seems, are two dangling pieces of art among the residue of life.

~

Monterey, Iraq, and Germany, 1972

Back in the United States, my mother's close friends were excited my parents weren't together anymore. They told her she deserved better.

She did deserve better. She knew that. After a year apart, she'd moved on.

But distance and time had the opposite effect on my father.

After Iraq, he was sent to work at a radio station in Germany. He spent weeks in cities he didn't know, walking through crowds of people who didn't speak his language. I imagine it occurred to him that he thought if my mother was with him, the long winter months wouldn't feel like drudgery. He missed her. He missed the way they worked together.

He loved her. The feeling crept up on him. It surprised him.

From whatever city he was in—Frankfurt or Berlin or was it Cologne?—my father wrote my mother a letter. It was an apology, a love letter, and a plea to give him another chance. He was smart enough to know that the only way to make sure she got his note was to send it to her mother in Monterey.

My father and my grandmother were friends. Back when he was still a student, he would go down to Monterey to visit her without my mother. This wasn't unusual; there was a spare key left outside, so my mother's friends could come and go, or stay when they needed to. These kids often came down to my grandmother's when they were homesick, needed to hide out, or wanted someone to listen to them. My grandmother always listened and never judged them.

So, she passed along my father's letter to my mother, and my mother lived with the note for weeks. She read and reread his words—words she never shared with me. She told me only that he'd said he was sorry and wanted to try again.

My mother softened enough that she agreed to pick him up from the airport when he returned from his year manning one radio station after another. For reasons I don't understand, no one was supposed to know he was back in the States. Only the ORC leaders knew, my mother, and hers.

My mother and father drove from the airport to my grandmother's house, three hours away. Maybe they stopped along the way and walked along that stony beach with the tide pools. Maybe they drove directly home. However it happened, they were together, properly this time, by the time they arrived at her door.

Is this when our family started?

EIGHT

United States, 1973–1976

By the mid-1970s, the Vietnam War protests were becoming American memories. Most of the American leftist groups—like the Weather Underground—had gone underground, dissolved, or imploded, while the US chapters of the Iranian Student Association, the Confederation of Iranian Students, and another group called the Federation of Iranian Students were more active than ever and were becoming increasingly militant. To the outside world, these groups seemed to work as a homogenous unit, but the reality was murkier. Internal politics were undercutting their unity. Revolutionary cells mushroomed, broke up, and reformed. My parents' group, the Organization of Revolutionary Communists, became the Union of Iranian Communists (UIC) by 1976 and numbered in the hundreds. Its members were scattered around the country. People even said there was a burgeoning arm of the UIC in Iran.

When the groups all worked together they were able to mobilize and organize protests and demonstrations, and get press to cover their events with speed and efficiency. By the middle 1970s, the American press confirmed that the SAVAK, the shah's secret police, was indeed spying on student activists abroad and across the United States. Reports also claimed that law enforcement agencies were cooperating with the shah's government and providing the names of political activists to the Iranian embassy.

My mother and father were in the middle of it all. My father was one of the highest-ranking leaders in UIC and a significant presence in the broader anti-shah movement, while my mother was in charge of press and communication for the Iranian Student Association. My father was a gifted recruiter who had spent years convincing students in Chicago, Illinois; Des Moines, Iowa; Lawrence, Kansas; Houston, Texas; and dozens of towns in between to join the movement. He now told these recruits that the movement, and the UIC, had presence across the United States and Europe and even in Iran.

Now was the time, he said, to become part of history, to organize and demonstrate and be disobedient. Working together, they could make the shah and his regime fall.

$$\sim$$

There are stories our parents tell us where the details are worn down with years of retelling, the edges are blunted and polished like the toe of a brass statue that's been touched over and over again by those rubbing it as they walk by. We the listeners learn the stories well enough that we assume the details, assume its fullness.

My mother's stories about the middle years of the 1970s were tossed off, blurred. I know my parents moved between Berkeley and Chicago, because she said that she liked the apartments in that cold city by a Great Lake. The spaces were big, and the crown moldings were ornate. But Ameh, my father's baby sister, remembers that when she visited them in Chicago, their apartment was small and the bed unmade. They were messy, Ameh said, which reminds me how young they were.

My mother said that she went to Germany at some point, and her perfect meal was bockwurst topped with sauerkraut and a golden lager to wash it all down. She never said why she was in Germany and

I didn't know enough to ask her. I didn't know to try and pull more story out of her, to ask her to say it again and again until I memorized it so I could tell you.

My mother's stories of her early years with my father were about how the two of them moved, unencumbered, around the world, "with just a toothbrush and a couple T-shirts." They enjoyed a kind of freedom I don't think exists anymore. It didn't when I was growing up, and it certainly doesn't now. There's no such thing as falling asleep so soundly at an airport gate, like my mother did one time during those years, that she missed plane after plane. When she woke up, twelve hours had passed by, and she grabbed her bag and she walked onto the next plane about to take off.

She dropped clues about their past like breadcrumbs. Children listen to stories like detectives, trying to figure out who their parents were, so they can understand who they, the child, might become.

I wonder if this is what you will do. I wonder how you will make sense of how we moved around a world that soon might sound different from your own.

~

Washington, DC, 2009

One day late in my mother's illness, when she was feeling especially sad, the two of us went for a walk on the National Mall.

She'd started hospice, and though she still had energy, the cancer was winning. It was a warm day, early in the fall as the leaves were just beginning to change. I sat her down under a tree and ran to the food cart to buy a sidewalk hot dog and a small Diet Coke. She wasn't allowed to eat or drink either thing, but I was focused on getting her to smile. I handed her the dog and soda, and we leaned against the tree, talking and watching the Canada geese terrorize tourists.

When we finished, my mother smiled, and exhaled.

"What else could one want from God?" she asked in Persian.

"Nothing," I said.

~

New York City, 1976–1977

Mahmoud stepped off a bus in Manhattan in July, a few days after the city's celebration of the United States Bicentennial had ended and all the tall ships that had filled the waters between Battery Park City and Ellis Island had sailed away. From Midtown, he walked to Harlem along streets that stank of rotting fruit, stale urine, and sour sweat. He found a cheap hotel where he rented a room for about $60 a month.

A member of the Chicago branch of the ISA, Mahmoud had traveled from the Midwest to New York to figure out how a group of Iranian and American students could chain themselves to the crown of the Statue of Liberty. Two or three times a week, he'd walk from his room down the length of Manhattan until he got to the southern tip of the island and aboard the ferry to the Statue of Liberty. He wandered the perimeter of the small island, glancing across the water toward the city on one side and the Verrazzano-Narrows Bridge on the other. He had six months to get the rhythms of Liberty Island and learn the ferry timetables.

Mahmoud took the elevator to the top of the pedestal, but he had to climb the rest of the way, up the steep and narrow double-helix stairwell that spirals into the statue's crown. Step by step, he went and passed the inverted face of the bronze lady until he got to the walkway in her crown. He was well over six feet tall, and the crown wasn't built for people his height. He ducked his head under the naked beams to see out of the rounded windows that make up the band of her seven-pointed crown.

The statue is thin-skinned—her bronze is only about the width of two pennies glued together. In the summer it holds in the heat like an oven, and when it's cold, the air howls around, blowing through her cracks.

Mahmoud looked around, trying to figure out how half a dozen activists, from the Confederation and an American group called the Revolutionary Student Brigade, could get up the stairs and chain themselves to the statue without raising alarms or being stopped.

This wouldn't be the first time Liberty Island had been host to political activity: the suffragists had used it as a symbolic backdrop for their demonstrations, and decades later the Vietnam Veterans Against the War did as well. President Lyndon B. Johnson even signed the Immigration and Nationality Act of 1965 on Liberty Island. But most of these groups had stayed on the island instead of entering the statue itself.

Mahmoud was planning a takeover of the statue, and it wouldn't be to demonstrate against the United States. They'd be striking against the Shah of Iran and in support of eighteen writers and intellectuals who'd been arrested in Iran, accused of being political dissidents. Many people, including those in the Confederation, believed that the trial would be a sham and the defendants would be executed. The protesters wanted both to embarrass the shah and his allies in the Jimmy Carter administration and to force the public to take notice.

Mahmoud was tasked with figuring out the logistics. Later, people like my father and mother would coordinate the protesters, vans, and motel rooms and come up with a strategy for negotiating with cops and speaking to the media.

Over the course of months, Mahmoud bought different kinds of chains and wrapped them around his midsection, taping down the links to mask the clinking of metal against metal. The chains were heavy and pulled at him. He went through several different kinds before he figured out how much he could carry and still walk normally. Once he decided on the type and length of chain, he went from one hardware store to another looking for the perfect lock, the kind that couldn't be cut with a standard bolt cutter. He found one finally that needed a diamond cutter to break through. The cops, he reasoned, wouldn't be able to bring the machine up into the statue's crown to cut them out.

By December, a few others had joined Mahmoud in New York. He led them through his plan, and they tweaked it. They put together two enormous banners, long enough to be seen from a distance and painted with two messages: one that read "Free the 18" and the other "Down with the Shah." The plan was to unfurl the fabric out of the statue's window, so it covered Lady Liberty's face.

A few weeks before the event was scheduled to take place in February, my father arrived in New Jersey and rented several rooms at a motel near the ferry landing. Soon the others trickled into town and started training for the demonstration. They wrapped themselves in chains and walked for hours until they grew used to the weight and pressure.

Just before the group was scheduled to pull their stunt, my mother joined them. Her job, as ever, was to talk to the press, hire lawyers, and negotiate with law enforcement. The group had come a long way since the *Chello-Yek Nafar* takeover. Now they expected consequences, both immediate and long-term.

The morning of February 15, 1977, everyone met at the motel and piled into the van and drove to the ferry launch. They spent the cold and cloudy morning playing tourist before, one by one, they'd walked up to the crown and barricaded themselves there. Someone told the tourists and the guards to leave.

Someone got a leg up to throw a length of chain over the bare bar that runs above the row of windows and then clicked the lock closed. The glass panes that made up the crown were broken, and their banners were shoved outside only to be caught in the wind, twisted, and made illegible. The Associated Press (AP) later reported that the National Park

Service did end up using bolt cutters to cut the group free because they had "misplaced the key," but I was told the protesters didn't misplace it. After they locked themselves in, one of them threw the key out of the broken window.

The takeover started around midday—it was probably then that two members of the ISA started calling the media. The AP said the protesters called their newsroom with a statement: "'We've just seized the Statue of Liberty, American and Iranian Students, which are members of the Revolutionary Student Brigade and the Iranian Student Association to protest the fact that a number of revolutionaries arrested in Iran are being held without trial and under torture.'" The report also cited the group's protest of the SAVAK's surveillance of Iranian students in the United States.

A spokeswoman for the ISA—likely my mother using an alias—was quoted in another AP article explaining the goal of the protest: "'Our demands are that the 18 be freed, their names be released, and that they be able to meet with an international delegation.'"[10]

Once the protesters were chained in and the press statements went out, my mother's next job began: negotiate the protesters' release.

She did.

The *New York Times* gave the protest a few column inches, and a federal judge issued a temporary restraining order banning them from the island and the statue. In a statement, the National Park Service described the outcome: "After the injunction was read to them there was a bit of bargaining. We've agreed to the amnesty—we'll not press charges—and they'll pay for all damages."

---

10 Associated Press. *"Statue Used for Protest by Iranians."* The Amarillo Globe-Times, February 16, 1977. https://www.newspapers.com/ image/29825935/. And: Associated Press. "Iranians Protest Torture." *The Eagle*, February 16,1977. https://www.newspapers.com/clip/77145368/ the-eagle/

The damages came to $308.

Not long after, I was told, the Iranian government released the eighteen prisoners, and by April, the shah allowed the International Red Cross to enter the country's prisons. They reported that there were about three thousand political prisoners held throughout the nation's eighteen prisons, a number that may have been much lower than in previous months, since the monarch had started releasing political dissidents before the IRC arrived.[11]

Those involved with the statue's takeover believed their protests not only helped bring attention to the myriad human rights violations and atrocities perpetrated by the shah's regime but also challenged the international community, especially the Carter administration, to continue to put pressure on the monarch to respect the rights and civil liberties of all his citizens.

I'm telling this story because my mother was incredibly proud of this moment. She often talked about the time that she and others chained themselves to the Statue of Liberty—she told my friends about it over and over again when we were growing up. It was an example of the best of life and all the good she was able to do with the Confederation.

But it's also an example of how I got too comfortable with the stories she told over and over, so comfortable I didn't ask her enough questions. I had a picture of what happened in my head: My mother and her friends stood with their arms linked around the circumference

---

11 William Branigin. "Rights Violations Under Khomeini Rival Shah's Era." The Washington Post, June 5, 1979. https://www.washingtonpost.com/archive/politics/1979/06/05/rights-violations-under-khomeini-rival-shahs-era/46b3ca52-2a87-4ebd-906c-426b9d46cd3f/

And: Robert C. de Camara. "The Shah as Tyrant: A Look at the Record." The Washington Post, March 23, 1980. https://www.washingtonpost.com/archive/opinions/1980/03/23/the-shah-as-tyrant-a-look-at-the-record/218c6a8e-dcb7-4168-ac9c-8f23609f888f/

of the statue. The wind was whipping their hair around as they shouted into the air.

～

Washington, DC, November 1977

Less than a year after the Statue of Liberty takeover, President Jimmy Carter welcomed the Shah of Iran to the White House for a state visit. The two leaders stood at the podium in front of the White House, speaking to gathered supporters and dignitaries about the special relationship between the two nations. Not far away an estimated three thousand people began to face off—about two-thirds were pro-shah, while the rest were anti-shah protesters who stood bunched along the edge of the White House lawn. As the president and the shah read their prepared remarks, the two groups clashed. Police threw tear gas into the crowd to break up the fighting. The wind picked up and blew the gas away from the fighting and into the faces of the president, the shah, and their guests.

With tears streaming down their faces, both President Carter and the shah tried to ignore the melee around them and kept talking over what was, at the time, the most violent demonstration to take place in DC since the Vietnam War. The next day's *New York Times* front page included a photo that captured a moment of chaos: placards and sticks being wielded by people in the crowd; in the foreground, an officer, his face screwed up in a grimace, shielding his face with one hand as a protester in a loose-fitting trench coat and black ski mask raises both arms.

The masked man was my father. His visage was frozen; his action incomplete.

My parents were two of the organizers of the demonstration. They handled the recruitment, transportation, housing, and press. Activists came from all over the United States.

"People say that this demonstration inspired the enormous protests in Tehran, the famous ones right before the shah's exile," my mother said. Thirty years later, my mother smiled when she told the story.

~

Midwest, August 1978

At least 377 people were dead—burned, asphyxiated, or trampled to death—after Cinema Rex, a movie theater in Abadan, a city in Iran, was set on fire. Hundreds more were injured trying to escape.

The papers blamed saboteurs and terrorists, while the government "refused to speculate about the exact identity of those responsible," and the shah suggested it was the leftists. Though, of the last, the *Washington Post* reported that "no evidence of such involvement has yet been produced." Much later, however, after the revolution, Islamists were found to be responsible for setting the fire and blocking the doors. They were prosecuted and subsequently executed. But in the days immediately following the tragedy, my parents and others believed the shah's government was responsible.

At a 1978 ISA meeting in either Iowa or Kansas, a young man stood up to talk about it. He said something about how someone had deliberately set the fire, locked the doors, and let the people burn.

As he spoke, he became more and more upset, working himself up so that he eventually started to shout that there was a fire in *their* building.

People got up and started to run out of the room; the meeting broke up.

Was the young man showing signs of mental illness or was he a SAVAK agent sent to sabotage the meeting?

They knew that group was being watched; everyone was sure of that, so when the scared man tried to run away, several men grabbed him.

Here is a story I was told: My father and a few others rented a cheap motel room where they brought the young man, tied him to a chair, and beat him, trying to get him to admit he was SAVAK. Or was he working with the US government? The FBI? The Iranian embassy?

Who?

Who was he working for?

In the story, my father's face went red as he shouted at the man, breathless with the effort. When it was over, my father and the others couldn't look at each other.

I don't know how true this story is or even if it's true at all. I will never know. All I know is something happened. When I asked Ameh about this incident she also didn't know the details. She said my mother mentioned it once but only said my father could never forgive himself for what happened in that room. He'd never done anything like it before and he never would again.

Here, again, is how we learn about the dead: through half stories told without the fullest context. And then we the living are left to reconcile the various incarnations of a person who isn't alive to speak for themselves. Without my father here, I have to accept what is potentially the whole of him: his darkest iteration to his lightest.

Now, I wonder, am I being disloyal sharing all of this with you?

PART II

NINE

Berkeley, California, 2018

Neda: Can you tell me a little bit about my father?

Speaker 2 (a former member of the Confederation): Okay. What do you want to know? He was very intellectual. He was very educated. He was a big influence on the whole Northern California branch. I learned a lot from him. He actually lived with us for a while and then we were so close. He was so nice. I loved him so much and always looked at him like a role model. Even when we went back to Iran, I still thought he was a good person, but he had his weaknesses.

Neda: Like what?

Speaker 2: He was fearful.

Neda: What was he scared of, do you think?

Speaker 2: I think he realized, once we got to Iran, that we had a smaller following in the country than we thought when we were in California. We were not as empowered as we thought. We were weak and . . . we couldn't find a "right" way. Nobody had the answer of how we could go forward. Your father was stuck, too, with no solution.

Neda: Yeah.

Speaker 2: He was very influential, but he was always a little bit . . . analyzing things rather than being part of the action. So, he was more a good analytic leader.

Speaker 2: Then there was one who could write very well. He had good theories about revolution. He was very educated. He and your father were on different sides. They had two different theories of how to go forward.

Neda: You're saying one group was about action and my father wasn't?

Speaker 2: He had a more passive approach. Maybe that would've worked better, who knows.

~

My father's master's thesis, published in 1968, is titled "An Evaluation of the Solutions of the Shortest Path Problem." His engineer's mind did not transfer to me, so when I opened those pages I didn't understand a word.

But from research, and the title itself, I think he was examining the problems that arise trying to get between two points. In the most basic sense, the shortest path between point A and B is a straight line, but that straight line may not always be the right choice.

Life and science are rarely simple. Often the points we try to connect aren't static; one point is heavier than the other, one point is seemingly more important. In life, these points are people and intention, history and imagination. They are goals—personal and public—we each strive for, the ones that shift and move about with circumstance and age.

The key to the Shortest Path Problem, it seems to me, is the ability to evaluate the situation quickly, take note when circumstances change, and move accordingly.

Doesn't that sound so easy?

Tehran, Iran, 1979–1982

The Iranian Revolution started two years before the shah fled the country on January 16, 1979. A month later, the monarchy finally collapsed and the Ayatollah Khomeini stepped off the plane, greeted by an adoring mass. When a reporter asked him how he felt being back after so many years in exile, the imposing cleric said he felt nothing.

But the thousands of Iranians who had been living abroad felt euphoric at the prospect of Iran without the shah. Planes out of California, New York, and cities across Europe were filled with Iranian students, activists, and revolutionaries, leftists and Islamists both. They spent the flights singing revolutionary anthems, and Amu, Ameh, and their many friends were among them.

My parents also returned, though separately. My mother remembered being stranded in a German airport for days after Khomeini, now the country's de facto leader, closed Iran's borders, including its airports. Iranian activists responded by protesting. They demanded the Ayatollah let a plane land in Tehran so that they could come home. The new leader did them one better—he sent a plane to pick them up.

My mother remembered the flight from Frankfurt to Tehran vividly. People were joyous. They had won another victory. When the plane landed on Iranian soil, the leftists fell to their knees and kissed the tarmac, while the Islamists hailed Allah and Khomeini. The divisions between those who'd been pushing for the same thing—the end of the shah's regime—were already starting to show. Soon they'd all watch this new Iran find its purchase. It would quickly transform, and they—the communists, the religious, and everyone else—would be forced to contend with all of it.

After both of my parents had arrived in Iran, my mother learned she was pregnant with me, but they didn't slow down their political activities. They leapt straight into the fray, spending long days in demonstrations and meetings with the Union of Iranian Communists. Comrades shouted from Tehran's street corners. Each day, my mother said, it seemed that another newspaper was founded, printed, and sold. People debated politics and argued with each other in public. Finally, my mother thought, there was a national dialogue.

Then, once Khomeini and his allies started to consolidate influence, what my mother had thought might be an exuberant new Iran was over. By the time I was born, in October 1979, Khomeini and his inner circle had locked down power, and arrests, executions, and torture were daily occurrences.

Khomeini's Islamists spent their first year in power dismantling all vestiges of the secular legal system and establishing an Islamic one. The Assembly of Experts revised the secular constitution into a strongly religious document that curtailed the rights of women and religious minorities. They arrested and executed dissenters en masse. Within months, the leftists in Iran started meeting in secret, staging demonstrations, and distributing literature deriding the policies of the new regime.

In an Iran shaken by revolution, however, the consequences of participating in protests or acts of civil disobedience were now higher, the desired outcome less obvious, and the punishments more severe. The activists didn't want another revolt. They wanted influence over the structure and institutions their new government was creating. But being inside the country meant they were vulnerable to arrest, interrogation, prison, and execution. And by now many had young children of their own. They weren't kids anymore; there was more to lose.

After my parents' return to Iran, my mother was embraced by my father's family and she became devoted to them in turn. Surrounded by aunts, uncles, siblings, cousins, and old friends, the loneliness and depression that had followed her through her childhood into her young adult years completely evaporated. Her relationship with my father also deepened, especially after I was born, another child of the revolution.

My father was, I've been told, besotted with me. He moved my crib to his side of the bed so that when I cried in the middle of the night, he could wake up to feed and comfort me, and my mother could sleep. These are the stories about my father that I hold on to; I turn them over as I try to understand what happened next: He loved me. He loved my mother. But he didn't put us first.

By the summer of 1981, dissatisfaction with the Islamic regime and its tactics had only intensified. A small faction within the Tehran chapter of the Union of Iranian Communists, called the Sarbedaran-e Jangal, proposed a plan for a violent uprising against the Islamic regime. My parents thought the plan reckless and opposed it. But the Sarbedaran moved forward, planning to stage the uprising in Amol, a small town by the Caspian Sea with a history of being sympathetic to leftist groups.

At one point, his comrades even kidnapped my father in an attempt to pressure him into supporting the idea, but they failed to convince him. Soon, however, the Sarbedaran faction won slight majority support within the UIC, and my father was removed from his leadership position. But he wouldn't leave the group, feeling responsible to the members he had recruited. My mother, for her part, had left the organization months earlier and dived into civilian life. She wanted my father to leave as well and focus on making a life for his family apart from politics. But she didn't want to make the choice for him. She hoped he would come to the decision in his own time.

On January 25, 1982, more than one hundred Sarbedaran fighters left their forest encampment and opened fire against government forces in Amol. The villagers didn't join the leftists as was hoped; they helped the regime. After about forty-eight hours of fighting, nearly every one of the insurgents was dead or under arrest. But the government had imposed a news blackout, so no one in the group knew exactly how many Sarbedaran had been killed or captured.

Those who hadn't gone to Amol knew that the captured fighters would eventually give up information about the organization and the names of its members. My parents' affiliation with the organization put our family in danger, so we and Ameh moved into a safe house, an unlisted apartment in central Tehran.

Amu and his wife, Shahrazad, who had also come back to Iran for the revolution, had been sent by the organization to another city north of Tehran to work in factories and help organize workers.

During our months in hiding, my mother spent her days teaching English at a language school she opened with a friend, and I stayed home with my father. He would spend hours telling me fantastic tales and drawing pictures to go with them. He made intricate wire sculptures, paintings, and wooden toys with secret compartments for me to play with. He rarely left the apartment except to visit family or exchange bits of information with organization members.

The spring of 1982, my mother was pregnant again. Our life then, she said, was surprisingly happy and calm, like the warm, quiet hours before a hurricane demolishes the shore.

Months passed. Still the Iranian government didn't retaliate or come to arrest those affiliated with the Amol uprising. One afternoon, as I played on the floor of the safe house, my parents talked about our future.

Have you thought about what would happen to her if we were arrested? my mother asked.

TEN

The morning we lost him, my father left the safe house dressed in the same gray trousers and light-blue button-down shirt he had worn to his thirty-eighth birthday party the week before. He had gained weight during his months underground, and the shirt buttons strained against his soft middle. He had a full beard, and his blue-green eyes shone beneath long, arched brows. He was heading to a meeting with several people who, like him, had been against the Amol uprising. No one in my family knew exactly where the meeting was to take place, but it must have been the same place they'd met previously, because Revolutionary Guards were waiting for them.

Here the story gets even hazier: Some people say they saw the Revolutionary Guards arrest my father on the street as he waited to cross; others say that the guards came into the meeting place and arrested the men together—catching them in the act. But everyone I spoke to agreed that the Revolutionary Guards weren't alone. They had brought along their informant—an old friend of my parents who was a member of the Sarbedaran and one of the planners of the Amol uprising—to identify my father and the others. The man pointed to my father and told the authorities his name and his position within the group. The guards, armed with automatic weapons, pulled my father's arms behind his back and bound his hands together at the wrists with rope.

Just before noon, my mother and I left her friend's apartment to meet my father at his parents' home. She had enrolled several new students in her language school, and she wanted to tell my father about them. She was six months pregnant, and she smiled as we walked.

The school might actually work, she thought. *It might become a real job with a steady income.*

But when we arrived at my grandparents' apartment, my father wasn't there. Other family members filtered through the apartment. Someone prepared lunch, and the television blared the World Cup final: Italy versus West Germany. My grandmother moved from room to room, talking at my grandfather in monologue as she finished packing for their weeklong trip to visit Amu, his wife, and their newborn daughter in Mashhad, a city in northeastern Iran. Minutes went by. No one except my mother noticed how late my father was. When lunch was ready, they did notice. They waited. Still he didn't come. My grandparents' train was scheduled to leave that afternoon. Reluctantly, they ate without him.

He's late, my mother said through clenched teeth. *He's late.*

Maybe he stopped somewhere to watch the match? Ameh said.

No one except my mother knew that he had gone to a meeting that morning. Though that wasn't unusual: my parents had always kept the specifics of their political work a secret from their family and friends. Ignorance allowed their loved ones some measure of plausible deniability. It also provided an added layer of safety: people couldn't reveal what they didn't know.

My mother kept an eye on the door and an ear out for the phone. On the television, soccer players raced up and down the pitch.

Why don't you come with us to the train station? Ameh suggested— anything to calm my mother and keep me occupied. My mother agreed.

In the car, my grandmother remembered she had forgotten to water the plants before she left. She asked Ameh to return to the apartment and water them, and then run upstairs and leave the keys with our cousin's husband, Ali. At the station, my grandparents got out of the car and made their way through the throng. We left the station and made a quick stop at the store before starting back toward my grandparents' apartment.

The afternoon was hot, and the car had no air conditioning. My mother and aunt had rolled down the windows, but the air wasn't moving, and the stop and start of traffic was pushing waves of sour exhaust inside. On the sidewalks, children with blackened fingers tried to sell rolled pieces of Hafiz's poetry—penny fortunes—to passersby. I sat quietly in the back as my mother drove Ameh back to my grandparents' apartment to water the plants.

Don't wait for me, my aunt said. *Go on home. Faramarz's probably there. I'll just walk or take a cab. I'll be there soon.*

As my aunt turned the key in the lock of the heavy steel door of the building, my mother pulled the car away. Ameh walked up three flights of stairs, unlocked the door, and stepped into the living room. Behind a long couch, the third doorway from the front door was Ameh's old room. It had a twin-sized bed, a chest of drawers, and a telephone. The line had been recently serviced, so the phone was unplugged, and the jack hung lifeless from the wall. The next room was the one my parents had stayed in when they first arrived in Tehran. After we had moved out, it was where I would sleep when dinners went on a long while, or when my grandmother took care of me. My toys were piled in the corners.

Ameh took off her headscarf and her overcoat before she walked into the kitchen, found the watering can, and began to make her way around the apartment. Around four o'clock, she finished watering the plants. She gathered her things and prepared to leave, shrugging into her long, faded green *roopoosh*, and arranging the beige silk scarf my father had given her. When the government had announced it would force women to wear hijab, my father had painted flowers onto women's headscarves and given them out, one by one, to family members. That afternoon she tied the ends of this scarf under her chin and reached for her keys. The intercom buzzed. She answered.

It's me, my father said. His voice sounded scratched and far away as it filtered through the call box into the receiver at his sister's ear.

I'm with the brothers, he said. My aunt laughed, thinking he was joking. "The brothers" was how people referred to the Revolutionary Guards.

Sure, you are, she said. *Sure, you're with the brothers.*

She was about to buzz my father into the building when she remembered that this was supposed to be a signal to hide anything in the house that was forbidden.

This is what we've planned for, she thought.

She placed the receiver on the table and moved through each room to make sure there were no outlawed newspapers, pamphlets, or books in the open. If there was anything to hide, she didn't see it. She picked up the receiver again.

Okay, she said. *I'll be right down.*

She grabbed the keys to the front door of the building and ran upstairs. She knocked quietly on our cousins' door. Ali answered, opening the door wide with a warm smile. She cut him off before he could speak.

Faramarz is here, she said, keeping her voice low. *He says he's with the guards. I don't know what's going on. If you don't hear from me, wait a little while and then come down.*

Then she hurried downstairs. As she pushed the heavy front door open, she saw her brother standing with his hands behind his back, as if he were waiting for the bus. It took a second for the scene to rush into focus. His hands were tied; his face resigned. He was surrounded by four Revolutionary Guards, each one holding an automatic weapon, at least one gun pointing at my father's back.

My aunt stepped back from the door to allow the men into the building. My father and the armed men entered. Inside the apartment, she offered the officers refreshments.

Some tea? she asked. *Or water?*

She had forgotten that it was the holy month of Ramadan and the sun was still up. Iftar wasn't for hours yet. The guards, each with a layer of dark stubble covering his face, declined her offer, admonishing her lack of piety with a look.

They sat my father down on a couch and began looking into the rooms. She couldn't tell the men apart. One asked where my parents' bedroom was. My father must have told them that this was where we lived. Ameh pointed toward the room with the crib, where I would sleep when my grandparents babysat me. While one guard stayed in the living room, the others worked their way from room to room, collecting and pocketing the family's passports, bric-a-brac, and random items of value like my grandfather's stamp and coin collections.

When the guards had taken whatever they wanted, they returned to the living room.

One guard looked at my aunt, but asked my father, *Who is she?*

She's young, my father said. *She's just in high school.*

The guard turned to Ameh and asked, *Where's Farah and the child?*

She's teaching, Ameh lied. My mother, of course, wasn't teaching. She was with me back in our apartment, waiting for either my aunt or my father to come home.

She'll be back soon, Ameh said.

The guards arranged themselves around the living room. They placed their weapons across their laps. The party of six—four guards, my aunt, and my father—sat together quietly and waited for my mother. Ameh noticed a warm light coming through the kitchen window. It was, she estimated, five o'clock in the afternoon when the phone rang.

My father was sitting close to his sister on one of the couches; his hands, still tied behind his back, forced him to slouch forward. His body was tense. She tried to read his expression—it wasn't shock, exactly. It was, she realized, defeat.

No one moved for a moment. The phone rang again and the guards told my aunt to answer it. Ameh stood up and crossed the room; she lifted the handset and spoke into the phone.

Is that Farah? the guards asked.

After a beat, Ameh shook her head no.

She replaced the phone on the cradle and returned to her seat by my father.

Was that Farah? my father asked Ameh under his breath.

She shook her head.

Several blocks away, my mother began to pace our apartment. It was after six o'clock, and my father still hadn't come home. Ameh wasn't back yet. I was playing with my doll. My mother sat on the floor near me and stared at the carpet, trying to figure out what to do. We didn't have a phone or a television; no one could reach us with news. The only sounds were my humming, her own heartbeat, and the noise of traffic from the streets below. She couldn't stay still anymore. She threw on her *roopoosh* and hijab. She took my hand and left the apartment for the phone booth down the street.

She dialed my grandparents' number, waited for the line to catch, the ring to sound, and someone to answer. The phone rang and rang. Just when she was about to hang up, she heard the soft click of the receiver being lifted.

Hello? she said. *Hello? Is that you? Why are you so late?*

Everything's okay, my aunt said. *We're okay.*

Behind my aunt's back, the guards were calling out, *Is that Farah? Is it Farah?*

They demanded Ameh show them where they could listen in on the call. She'd pointed them toward her old room, and they all rushed to reassemble the unplugged extension.

Why are you still there? my mother asked. *What's going on? What's taking so long?*

Everything's okay, my aunt said. *The brothers are here.*

For who? my mother asked. *Who did they come for? For you? For Faramarz?*

They're not here for me, my aunt said. *Everything's okay. Faramarz said you should go and drop the children at your mother's house now, then come over.*

It was after eight o'clock. My mother stood in the phone booth, one hand pressing the handset to her ear, the other gripping mine.

"Drop the children at your mother's." It was a message from my father to my mother: Our home wasn't safe anymore. Iran wasn't safe anymore. In order to save our family, my mother had to get back to California with my unborn brother and me.

By the time the guards had the phone working, the call was over. They walked back into the living room, their guns at their sides.

What did she say? they asked.

She's on her way here, my aunt said.

The six adults again settled into their seats. Ameh pushed herself closer to my father and whispered, *I told her what you said. I told her to take the children to her mother's.*

My father's body relaxed.

The guards got up and began to search the rooms again, more out of boredom than anything else. My father leaned toward my aunt.

The government has a list of names, he said. *They're going to start arresting everyone on the list. Tell people to get out.*

Members of the organization knew not to share any information with interrogators for at least twenty-four hours after their arrest. The delay would give the others who weren't caught in the dragnet a chance to get away or go into hiding. After a day, if the questioning and torture became too much, the detained could give information—my father gave up one person. Decades later, I was able to speak to that man's wife, and she held my hand and told me she didn't blame my father.

Out on the street, my mother walked out of the phone booth and half pulled me behind her as she hurried back to our apartment—the safe house where we'd been living for months.

She grabbed a plastic bag and stuffed in my birth certificate, my father's green card, her college transcripts, whatever she could find. She grabbed a change of clothes for me and threw that in over the pile of papers. She picked me up and left the apartment. She walked down to the street and then stopped to think.

She considered the people she knew who might take the risk of letting us in and helping us figure out what was happening to my father. She decided to walk to my father's cousin's house. Esmet opened the door, dressed for a dinner party, with her husband, Jafar, standing behind her—the sun had set and people were gathering for iftar. They looked at my mother, holding on to me with one hand and with the other, the bag filled with children's clothes and papers.

They have Faramarz, my mother said as they ushered her inside.

My mother told them what little she knew, and they offered to go to my grandparents' apartment and act as if they were dropping in for a quick visit, a tea and a biscuit to break the fast with the family.

As Esmet and Jafar were leaving my mother and me, our cousin's husband, Ali—the one who lived upstairs—knocked on my grandparents' apartment door. When a guard answered, Ali apologized for disturbing them, explaining politely that he was just there to see his family.

Who is this? the guard asked my aunt.

He lives upstairs, she said.

The guard stepped back and Ali walked in, nodding to each guard in turn before greeting my aunt and father.

I just came down to say a quick hello, he said as he took one of the empty seats in the living room.

No one responded. Time passed. It was about nine o'clock in the evening. The intercom for the front door sounded. Everyone looked up. My father and aunt had been certain my mother had gotten the message.

Warily, my aunt lifted the receiver for the front door.

Hello? She said.

Hello! Esmet's voice called out. My aunt buzzed her in.

It is our other cousin, my aunt told the guards. *We've missed iftar, I think.*

She opened the door and invited Esmet and Jafar to have a seat in the living room. My aunt then excused herself to the kitchen to make tea. She set the tray for eight people and laid out a plate of fruit and sweets. They all sipped tea from my grandparents' delicate glass tea cups.

The guards aren't vicious, Ameh thought. *They haven't hit us or yelled. They've been civilized about it, really.*

Then she thought, *Oh God, this is it. It is all over. It is all done.*

It was midnight before the guards gave up waiting. They pulled my father from the couch and gave him a moment to say goodbye to his sister. My aunt and father held each other. For the first time that night, Ameh cried.

After the siblings parted, the guards led my father down the stairs and onto the street. It would be more than a month before we had any news of him—broadcast over a Radio Tehran news report we would hear in the hotel lobby in Turkey. That would be the first time the government publicly acknowledged that they had him—but that was still weeks away.

My aunt closed the door, then turned and looked at her cousins; the four of them listened to the footsteps and then the sound of the heavy front door closing.

ELEVEN

Tehran, Iran, August 8, 1982

It was nearly five o'clock in the morning when Amu woke my six-year-old cousin, Laleh, to say goodbye. He left her his calligraphy pen and asked her to keep it safe for him until he could come back for it. She nodded sleepily and promised that she would. She kissed him before falling back to sleep. In the other room, my mother, aunts, and uncles were gathering the last of our belongings and arranging them in the trunk of the car, while Laleh's older brother, my cousin Asef, wailed.

Why can't I come? he asked, tears streaming down his face. He was eight years old and knew a long road trip meant picnics, and picnics meant freshly grilled kebabs.

I want to come, too! he screamed, inconsolable. *I want kebab!*

For goodness' sake, his mother said. *No one is going to eat kebab without you.*

~

When my father's older brother, Farid, first contacted the smugglers to get us out of Iran, they promised we would make the journey to Turkey by car. It would be a long trip, but a relatively simple and straightforward one: an eight-hour drive from Tehran to Tabriz, a city near the Turkish border. From there, a five- or six-hour drive to the border, where another car would pick us up and we'd drive to Van, a Turkish border city.

My mother was seven months pregnant and worried that the long car rides would be dangerous. She wouldn't agree to the plan until her doctor assured her that, as long as she took breaks whenever possible, a car ride wouldn't hurt the baby or herself. They'd both be fine. If the pressure in her legs became too painful, he prescribed Valium to help relax her muscles. My mother's fears assuaged, she agreed that she and I would come.

My mother then convinced my grandfather to send his youngest daughter, Ameh, over the border with us. She promised him that Ameh would be safe with us. Then she insisted that Amu and his wife, Shahrazad, who was also political, and their five-month-old baby leave with us as well and not wait for the Revolutionary Guards to knock at their door. The guards who were aggressively arresting anyone even distantly affiliated with the Amol uprising.

Once everyone had agreed on who would leave the country, my family paid the smugglers half of the almost $30,000 US dollars they demanded—the equivalent of $81,000 in 2021 dollars. The price included the cost of five passports to replace those the Iranian government had confiscated the day the guards arrested my father. It was agreed that the smugglers would get the second half of the money once they brought my family proof that the six of us had arrived safely in Turkey.

There is a photograph from the night before we left. In it, I'm standing on the edge of the living room, watching anxiously as my mother, aunts, and uncle stuff clothes and documents into large suitcases. I wasn't allowed to bring most of my clothes, so, piece by piece, I'd carefully put on my favorite items in order to wear them one last time: a sparkling costume vest over a favored dress and shiny pants. I looked on as the adults worked. Somewhere in the pile of clothes was the blue windbreaker I took with me everywhere. With one hand, I would hold the jacket and rub the fabric rhythmically while I sucked my thumb. The noise and feel of the ridged material were familiar and comforting.

The day we left, my father had been gone for exactly one month. No one had acted normally since he left. They were distracted and harried. They disappeared for days at a time.

The morning of our escape, my mother woke me before daybreak. She helped me into my clothes and we walked out to the car. I climbed onto my uncle's lap and curled into him. Shahrazad sat beside him, holding their baby. My mother sat on my uncle's other side, while my aunts, Ameh and Minna, were pushed against each other in the front seat. Minna's husband was driving.

The engine turned over and a song began to play about a woman whose heart had split in two: half she was taking with her and the other half she had left behind with her lover. When the song ended, my mother asked my aunts to rewind the cassette and play it again. And then, again. The song played over and over. No one wanted to hear anything else.

They didn't speak very much during the drive that morning. My aunt Minna told Ameh not to eat any yogurt during the journey.

It won't be pasteurized, she said, *and you could get very sick.*

~

Near the halfway point in the journey between Tehran and Tabriz, my uncle pulled the car onto the side of the road. Our family climbed out, all of us unfolding ourselves and stretching our limbs long so the blood could rush to our skins' edge. Someone laid a blanket on the grass and we looked like a family on a summer holiday, stopping for lunch.

When we'd finished eating, we folded ourselves back into the car and continued to drive northward. A couple of hours later, the car blew out a tire and the minutes ticktocked. Someone walked to a nearby town where we could buy a new tire to replace the flattened one. When we finally arrived in Tabriz to meet the smuggler, it was 4:00 p.m. We were three hours late to meet him. He was furious.

The smuggler was called Nariman. He was unshaven and had thick black eyebrows that met in a dark furrow over his nose. He told my uncle to follow his car to Khoy, another town several hours away. There we would meet the men who would take us to the border. When we got there, however, the men had long since left. Nariman told us to get into his car; he would take us to Salmas, yet another town, where he would find someone to help us.

While Nariman transferred our luggage from my aunt and uncle's car into the trunk of his own, my mother and the others said goodbye to my aunt Minna and her husband. Then, we climbed into Nariman's car and he peeled away, barreling southward down the dark road.

When Minna got back into her car, she looked into the back seat. In the commotion, we had left the baby's bag filled with formula and diapers.

It is too late, she thought miserably. The smuggler's taillights had long since disappeared into the night.

~

As the smuggler sped us toward Salmas, Ameh gripped the seat back, terrified. The road was unlit except for the glow from the car's headlights as we raced around the turns and gunned down the straightaways. It was after 2:00 a.m. when he finally stopped in front of a house. A tall, wiry man called Asad opened the door and ushered our group inside, careful that no one should see us. He wouldn't let us bring our luggage inside and berated Nariman for being late to meet the horses. My mother, aunts, and uncle exchanged looks.

The horses? someone asked Asad. *What do you mean "we missed the horses"?*

Of course, horses, Asad said, his voice cold. *Did you think you'd be smuggled out of the country in a car? I did wonder why you brought a pregnant woman and an infant.*

He paused to consider us.

Don't worry, he said, his tone lighter. *It's only a couple of hours' ride, then a car will meet you at the border to take you the rest of the way.*

He smiled.

I don't do this work for the money, he said. *This is my service to God.*

He gave us tea and bread and told us to rest a while. At about four o'clock in the morning, he woke us. My aunt Shahrazad took one of his old sheets and tore it into strips to fashion a diaper for the baby. One of the smugglers led us to a car idling in the alley next to the house. He drove us to a large park in a neighboring town, where we were to wait until nightfall.

For hours my family wandered the garden's grounds. I napped in the car. The driver took Shahrazad and Ameh into town to buy shoes and food. After sundown, he drove us back to Asad's house to change for the journey. Asad handed my mother and my aunts several sheepskin bags and told them to transfer what they could from our suitcases. When they complained that our clothes would stink of livestock, he laughed.

You certainly can't take those suitcases with you, he told them.

Finally, his men drove us to the outskirts of town and told us to get out of the car and walk along a tall wall that bordered the town. We were to stick close to the shadows.

We'll reach the horses in twenty minutes, they said.

We saw jagged mountain peaks piercing the far-off horizon. The sky was inky black. My aunts couldn't see and kept tripping over the rocks and losing their footing in the divots along the path. Shahrazad's new shoes ripped apart.

After a while, the smugglers told us to be still and hush. Someone had seen a light in the distance. The town's patrolman was coming toward us.

I need to pee, I said, whining at first and then starting to panic as everyone told me sharply to stay quiet and not make a noise. The patrol passed us by. Minutes later, when the smugglers were sure he was gone, I was allowed to relieve myself.

We walked on. An hour passed. Then another half hour. I became too heavy to carry. I had to walk, and someone held my hand. Like the bulky luggage, I must have slowed us down. As my family walked around me, I held on to my blue jacket and I tried to stay quiet for the rest of the long, strange night.

~

At 10:30 p.m. we arrived at the horses. Each of us was paired with one smuggler, who helped lash our bags over the packhorses' backs. The man who rode with my mother helped her climb onto her animal. She had to stretch her left leg over one bag and her right leg over the other. Without the use of her thighs to help her stay in place, she was at the mercy of the animal and the smuggler. She gripped the saddlebags with both hands.

Ameh and Amu helped Shahrazad zip the baby inside her quilted jacket—a light shell better suited to cool summer nights than an overnight horseback ride over frigid mountain peaks.

I remember nearly nothing from the journey, just shadows and impressions. I do remember wanting my mother that night. I remember that when she told me I couldn't be with her, I was confused and wondered if I were in trouble. I didn't understand that there wasn't enough room for me on her horse. I didn't understand that she was too big, the horse too small, and the trail too dangerous.

Now I also wonder if the last thing my mother would have wanted just then was a child pressed up against her. To be strong for me, she needed space from me. I was given my own horse and my own mustachioed smuggler. He scared me, so Ameh and my uncle let me ride with them at various points in the night, but I don't remember that at all. I held on tightly to my blue satin jacket.

The night went on. Ameh's horse wandered from the rest of ours.

Don't be scared, the smuggler riding with my aunt told her. *You're like a sister to me. I'll take care of you.*

It grew later still. The horse swayed beneath me. I fell asleep against the smuggler. In my sleep, my fingers loosened their grip on my windbreaker. I woke up when it fell from my hand, floating down the mountainside. I begged the smugglers, my mother, aunts, and uncle to stop the horses and go back and find it. My smuggler went back and tried, but he didn't see it.

I know where it is, I told him. *I can find it.*

But it was dark and late. We had to keep moving. The moment they stopped looking for my jacket, I filled up with a fear so profound, the rest of me shrank to nothing.

The world is unfair, and I am washed away. I remember that feeling clearly.

~

It was around 3:00 a.m. when the smugglers led us to a barn where we could rest for the night. Someone had laid out five mattresses for us on the barn floor. The men slept on the floor at our feet. In the morning, they brought us cups of dirty tea, bowls of yogurt, hot oil, and a plate of bread. As we tore off sections of bread and wiped them across the clotted layer of animal fat, the smugglers began to argue with us about their fee. They claimed Asad's men hadn't paid them what they were promised. They stabbed the bread into the hot oil to punctuate their point. They wiped their mustache bristles with the backs of their hands. My mother, Amu, and Ameh said that we had already paid a fortune, and couldn't pay any more.

~

Hours passed. Inside the barn, the air was heavy, itchy with dust and dander and hay. Two days before, the smell of horses, humans, and shit would have overwhelmed us, but now it barely registered. Mice ran over the tops of the mattresses. Shahrazad held her daughter. For two days, she had tried to keep one hand clean to coax her daughter's mouth to her breast, but her daughter wouldn't suckle.

The packhorses snorted and slouched in the stables next door; the smugglers had gone off to find another horse for my mother so she could ride alone.

Throughout the afternoon, the men came and went, speaking to each other as if we weren't there, their voices low and guttural. They were trying to figure out how to get more funds from us before we had to leave that night.

Late afternoon, the light leaking through cracks in the stable's walls shone orange and red. There was little water left and none of it clean, but we drank what we had. The baby fussed and her face turned red. Her small body tensed, and her fists curled. Dehydrated and exhausted, she cried while my aunt tried, again and again, to feed her. Once night fell, the men came for us.

~

The third night, the smugglers promised we were close to the border.

Every half hour, they said, *See the rise in the distance? The city of Van is just beyond that hill. That's where we're going.*

As we came closer, the terrain became more hazardous and the official checkpoints multiplied. Within a mile or two of each checkpoint, they made us get down from the horses and walk with a guide in one direction, while the rest of them led the horses in another. Then we'd all meet again a mile or so past the checkpoint and climb back on to the horses and begin the ride again. Then came another checkpoint, and we'd do it all again.

At the first checkpoint, Shahrazad broke my mother's Valium into shards and fed a small sliver to the baby so she would stay quiet as we made our way. The baby had started shitting herself and my aunt was nearly out of her makeshift diapers. The baby was sick and tired. Each time we stopped, my aunt would tear the rags into smaller pieces to clean and diaper her daughter.

The night went on. We climbed higher. The air got colder. The horses began to pick their way over packed snow and ice. My baby cousin's face began to turn blue. At each stop, my uncle would put his hand close to his daughter's mouth to feel if she was breathing.

~

My mother was uncomfortable as she rode through the night. Her legs, propped up over the sheepskin bags, kept losing sensation. Whenever we had to stop, she had to be lowered from the horse and Ameh would rub her calves and thighs until she could feel her legs again. Her backside was skinned and bruised, and she had hemorrhoids, which the long hours on the horse aggravated. The pain, she later said, was indescribable.

At some point that night, my mother's horse slipped, her breath caught, and her heart spiked. She gripped the reins, adrenaline coursing through her veins.

This is dangerous, she thought. *It's exciting. If Faramarz were here, it would be fun. It would be an adventure that we'd remember and laugh about.*

He should be here, she thought.

Turkey came closer, Iran yawned at our backs, and a heaviness settled over my mother. The sky lightened; she could just make out the small village in front of her. She didn't feel relief, only the beginning of grief pushing against her throat.

~

By the fourth morning we were covered in dirt. Shahrazad's shoes had already fallen apart, and now so had my mother's. The smugglers led my family through the village. Yellow lanterns lined the streets. Under their glow, it was easy to forget the town was deep in the heart of a lawless borderland.

The Kurdish smugglers left us at a short, squat house, and another set of smugglers—this time all Turkish men—met us there. Exhausted and sore, my mother, aunts, and uncle entered the house and waited in the hallway. My mother's legs shook. Ameh held my hand. My uncle was quiet, while my aunt Shahrazad, who spoke Azerbaijani Turkish, tried to listen to the smugglers' conversation without letting on that she could understand. She wanted them to speak freely in front of us.

The smugglers' house had two rooms, and in one, nearly twenty women were sitting together. Some young, others old and weathered. As my mother watched them from the hallway, she remembered a scene from *Zorba the Greek*. In that movie, a woman is dying in a dusty village and all the other women are watching her pass away. When she finally dies, the women, dressed in black, resembling a murder of crows, fall over themselves trying to grab at everything she left behind.

My mother thought these women looked at us the same way. The only difference was these women were dressed in white with colorful scarves tied around their heads and waists. A few detached themselves from the group when they saw us staring. They led us into the next room and left our bags in the hallway. As my mother, aunts, and uncle eased onto cushions on the floor, they heard the women begin to rummage through our things. Later we found they had stolen clothes, Ameh's contact lenses and case, and the leather purse my mother had given her on her eighteenth birthday. They also took the last of the makeshift diapers.

My mother was tired.

Once they take their fill of our stuff, she thought, *one of them will bring us some water or tea; maybe they'll let us sleep for a few hours.*

The Turkish smugglers walked into the room where we sat. They stood shoulder to shoulder and blocked the doorway.

The smugglers said they wanted more money. My family reminded them that we had an agreement and that we didn't have any more money to give. If we couldn't wrestle up more cash, the smugglers threatened to leave us to make our own way.

Fine. Leave us, if that's what you want, said my mother, aunts, and uncle, frustrated.

The smugglers yelled. They threatened; they cajoled. My mother, aunts, and uncle were hungry, thirsty, and exhausted, but somehow they dug in and refused.

The smugglers left the room. After a few minutes, they returned.

Okay, one of them said. *We'll take you, but we have to leave now.*

They didn't wait for nightfall.

~

A boxy red sedan idled outside the house. The smugglers threw what was left of our belongings into the trunk, while my family—four adults and two small children—climbed into the back seat. Three smugglers got into the front. One was driving, and the other two pushed next to each other in the passenger seat. They drove us out of the village into a dry, desertlike clearing. The driver stopped the car and told us to get out.

One by one, my family climbed out of the car. The adults thought it was the same stop-and-start from the night before. They braced themselves for another long trek around a Turkish checkpoint. It was hot; the cold mountain peaks felt very far away.

We waited for the smugglers to tell us where to go and how far we should walk. But they didn't. They drove away and we were left on the roadside, alone.

~

The sun was relentless. We were surrounded by miles of flat land with scattered rocks and a paved road that wound over the surface. We didn't have water or a map. Not knowing what to do, we sat down and waited for the smugglers to return. The baby began to cry. Shahrazad spit into the infant's mouth and used her body to shield her daughter from the sun.

An hour passed, maybe more. As the sun moved farther across the sky, I began running in circles and throwing my body against the ground. I started speaking gibberish; my face grew red, hot, and dry to the touch. My eyes were unfocused, darting right and left. It was heatstroke.

My mother tried to calm me, but I wouldn't be calmed. I was dehydrated, scared, and exhausted. The baby was crying.

I'm going for help, my mother said.

Shahrazad, as the Turkish speaker, said she'd go, too. The two women walked up to the road. They looked down the two-lane highway. They saw waves of heat rise up from the asphalt.

A long time passed before they heard the sound of an engine and saw a truck coming toward them. They started to wave their arms. Their desperation made them careless.

The truck could have been anyone's, but from the moment we had crossed the border into Turkey, my mother believed that her American citizenship would protect her and me. Even if the Turkish border patrol caught us, they couldn't send us back to Iran. She thought they might deport us to America. The thought made her reckless.

The truck belonged to the Turkish state's electricity company. Inside were a couple of electricians on their way to a small village to work on a government electrification project.

My aunt leaned into the window to speak to the men.

We're in trouble, she said in simple Azerbaijani Turkish. *Please help us.*

My aunt and mother pointed back toward Ameh, Amu, the baby, and me. They pantomimed heat and thirst. They tried to communicate that we were in danger.

We've been abandoned, Shahrazad told the men in the truck.

In simple Turkish, the electricians said they couldn't bring us with them to the remote village, but they would come back for us.

If you're still here, the men promised, *we'll help you.*

They drove away. The women walked back to us.

~

I had collapsed in Ameh's lap. My uncle was holding the baby. Shahrazad and my mother were telling them about the truck when they heard the sound of a car. They watched the car pull off the road and stop near us. Two men got out and walked toward us.

For a fee, one said, *we can get you to Van.*

My mother blanched when she heard his price. My mother told my aunts and uncle to go with these new smugglers.

If someone catches us here, she said, *they'll send you back to Iran. You can go with these guys, you probably should, but I won't. I'll stay here, wait for the electricians to come back, or I'll hitchhike. Someone will come.*

My aunts and uncle decided the baby was too sick to take a chance on the electricians returning. They told the new lot of smugglers that they would go with them. Just then, the red sedan drove up. Our old smugglers jumped from the car and ran toward us. They had been watching us from somewhere. They screamed and shouted at this new group of smugglers to leave us.

My mother, aunts, and uncle watched the old and the new smugglers argue and threaten each other. It was nearly dusk. The heat was breaking. The old smugglers paid off the new ones to leave us behind. We crammed back into the red sedan and drove away.

~

It was night. It was dark. At the checkpoints, my mother, aunts, and uncle carried the baby as they walked around the guards' station. But I was too heavy for anyone to carry and I was too exhausted to walk, so I stayed in the car with the smugglers. My family had to trust that the smugglers wouldn't take me.

It was sometime before midnight when the smugglers said we had come to another checkpoint.

Get out, they said.

My family got out of the car and this time I climbed out with them. The smugglers took our luggage from the trunk and left it on the road. Then they climbed back into the car and drove away. For the second time that day, my mother, aunts, and uncle watched the taillights of the red sedan recede.

This time the smugglers didn't come back for us.

My family looked around. There were no streetlights. There were no road signs. It was completely quiet. They didn't know which direction led toward Iran and which went farther into Turkey. They tried to decide which direction to go.

In the dark, it was impossible to tell how fast time was passing. It might have been ten minutes, it might have been an hour, but finally they heard the sound of a truck in the distance. Someone took my hand. Shahrazad made sure the baby was secured to her side. My mother bent over the remnants of the bags they had carefully packed just a few nights before. She took out papers and rags they could use for baby diapers. My aunts and uncle took what they could and we began to walk slowly toward the traffic noise.

This was the third night without sleep. Shahrazad couldn't hold the baby anymore. She gave her to Amu and tried to concentrate on walking. She lifted her foot and fell over like a plank, face-first. My mother pulled Shahrazad to her feet and slapped her hard. My mother pushed

Shahrazad to move. Then, it happened again. My aunt fell forward, fast asleep. Ameh pulled Shahrazad up. My mother slapped her across the face and pushed her to walk forward.

The moon was a curved crescent that night. We were walking over loose rocks and soil, trying to stay close to the road. At one point, my mother slipped on the broken rocks that dissolved into dust with pressure. She hadn't realized that the shoulder had narrowed to a sliver that separated the road from a steep incline. She lost her footing and fell down on her stomach and she kept falling until she came to the bottom. My mother pushed herself to her knees and felt her way up to the road.

She tried not to think about the baby in her belly; she could not think about him. She brushed herself off and continued to walk on and on until dawn began to break. As the sky lightened, we were able to see our surroundings. On the opposite side of the road, my family saw our first road sign. We crossed the highway to read it: "Van 10 km." Ten kilometers, back in the direction we had come. But at least, for the first time in days of walking, riding, and climbing, my family knew where we were going.

We arrived in Van a few hours later. We were dirty, shattered, thirsty, and shoeless. But somehow, my family walked into town on our feet.

~

We walked until we found the hotel, and when we entered the building, the staff was amazed.

How did you get into the city? a clerk asked. *How did you get here without someone from the military seeing you? You should've been picked up,* he said, impressed. *You should've been arrested and sent to the detention center.*

My mother, aunts, and uncle were too tired to think how lucky they'd been. The staff told them they had to go to the police station and register; the officers would take their passports and they'd have to bribe them. Then they could come back to the hotel to bathe and rest.

You don't have a choice, the clerk said. *Everyone does this.*

But this isn't part of our plan, someone in my family explained. *We'll only be in Van for a few days.*

But the clerk insisted: *Make it easier on yourselves, go to the police now.*

So, we did. My mother and Shahrazad walked carefully, barefoot, trying to step over the cracked bits of street. My uncle was lost in his thoughts, as he had been most of the journey. He had helped with the baby. He had helped with me. He had made nervous jokes. He was twenty-seven, the only man of the party, and equal parts scared and angry. It wasn't supposed to be like this. He was a revolutionary, not a refugee. Revolutionaries were supposed to fight and win or fight and fall.

～

At the station, the police took my family's information and confiscated their papers. They wanted cartons of cigarettes as payment to ensure a message, a note, or a form would make it through the winding bureaucracy to the appropriate office. The officers sat behind their desks sipping from glasses of sweet tea.

Whatever my family asked about was declared impossible, until cigarettes or other bribes were produced. Then the officers nodded, and then the form was moved along the chain of command. Applying the right bribe to the right official was as important as filling out the paperwork correctly.

My mother looked around the station and considered her situation. The best chance she had to get out of Van was to use her pregnancy. She was now nearly eight months pregnant. She told an officer that the stress and strain of the journey had started her contractions.

I need to leave Van before the baby comes, she told the officer, using Shahrazad as her translator. The officer looked at my mother; she was covered in sweat, dust, and dirt, but her voice was strong.

You're in labor, are you? he asked.

She nodded.

Okay, he said. *Fine. Don't worry. Let's go to the hospital. We have everything you'll need there. You can have your baby there.*

The officer led my mother to the local hospital, a small building with a few rooms branching from a hallway. Shahrazad came with her as a translator and to see if she could get diapers and medicine for her baby. The women were shown to a room with what looked like an old dentist's chair in the corner.

Crouched on either side of the chair were two nurses holding a young woman's legs open. The woman in the chair wore a tribal head-dress. Her skirts were hiked up. My mother watched as a nurse bent down in front of the woman; when she straightened, she was holding a newborn.

After the nurse laid the baby down, she helped move the woman into another room with bare mattresses set up on top of cots. From a distance, my mother saw that the baby's swaddling was stained with dirt. The nurses brought the mother her baby, then returned to my mother and aunt.

Okay, one of the women said to my mother, motioning toward the chair. *Sit down, you need to be examined.*

The chair has blood all over it, my mother said.

The nurse took some towels and old rectangles of cut canvas from a pile in the corner of the room and spread them over the chair.

You can't examine me until you clean and disinfect that chair, my mother said.

The nurses clicked their tongues and looked disapprovingly at the two dirty Iranian women standing in the doorway. My mother and aunt stared back.

The nurses threw more towels over the chair. They gestured impatiently for my mother to come forward. My mother and aunt retreated.

As they walked through streets filled with people, animals, and cars spewing exhaust, my mother knew she needed to get out of Van quickly, or she'd be back there in that hospital.

~

After my mother and Shahrazad returned from the hospital, my family separated into two groups: my mother, Ameh, and I took one room with two narrow beds. Amu, Shahrazad, and their baby took the room with a single bed and a telephone.

That night, for the first time in five days, we all bathed. Then, while my mother went to lie down, the others took me and went to find food and supplies.

My mother stared out of the window to the bazaar below, watching people buy fruit and vegetables from the stalls. She noticed a stand that sold shoes and reminded herself she needed to buy a new pair in the morning.

She was alone for the first time in days. She stretched out over the bedcovers and closed her eyes. She was too tired to sleep. She thought about my father. She felt heavy.

Is this grief? she wondered. She thought of her unborn son; she thought of me. She realized she didn't feel anything—no joy, no anticipation.

I want Faramarz, she thought. *Does he think I abandoned him? Does he know that I don't have anything without him? I have to get back to Iran. How will I get back to Iran?*

Her thoughts moved fast, then faster. She opened her mouth to pull air in, but she couldn't. There was no air in the room. She tried to calm herself. She promised herself that she'd get back to Iran. She'd give birth to my brother in the United States and get us settled in our

American lives, and then in a year's time, she'd go back to Iran the same way we got out.

The room was too small, and she needed space. She got to her feet and tried the door. She pulled at the handle. It didn't give.

I'm trapped, she thought. *I can't breathe, and I'm trapped.*

She pounded on the door over and over.

Let me out! she screamed. *Please! Let me out!*

Pounding and screaming, pounding and screaming—her thoughts circled back: *I'm trapped. I'm in prison. This room is a cell. I'm trapped. I'm in prison. This room is a cell. I'm trapped. I'm in prison. This room is a cell.*

Finally, she heard footsteps, and the door opened. Air rushed in. My aunts and uncle were there. They hadn't left her.

"That was the nearest I got to losing it," my mother said, years later. "It was claustrophobia, but also my heart was breaking. My heart was bursting was what it was."

~

In 1982, Van, an old city along Turkey's eastern border, was full of Iranian refugees. The other guests at the Hotel Kent, many of whom were families like ours, had been smuggled out of the country, too. But my mother said that most weren't political refugees—most weren't running from their past. They were normal people fed up with the Islamic regime; they were scared of the ongoing Iran-Iraq War. Many left Iran without having contacts outside of the country. Their motivation for leaving was simply that they had had enough, or they were afraid, or they wanted something else for their lives. They packed up their belongings and gathered their savings and then ran for the hills, often with children in tow.

Turkey was our way out, as it was for thousands of Iranian refugees who left over those hills in those years. Each one was required to report to the local police for processing. Each was told to surrender their passport and other documents and give a plausible reason for having left home. If they didn't voluntarily report themselves to the authorities, more than likely they'd be hauled into the station by Turkish police monitoring the refugee hotels. If that happened, the refugees would find themselves in a detention center or deported back to Iran.

The first few days in Van, my mother noticed, many newly arrived Iranians became visibly lighter and happier. Women shed their hijabs and the full-length *roopoosh* and men raced to the bar and to playing cards.

But this wasn't freedom: Turkish soldiers stood guard with loaded automatic rifles on every street. Many Iranians weren't allowed to leave their hotels, and no one was allowed to leave Van until a background check was complete. The entire process could take at least two months.

For many, the initial giddiness of being out of Iran gave way to despair and desperation. These were people trapped in purgatory. They'd paid exorbitant fees, both at home and along their journey over the border, so by the time they arrived, their funds were depleted. While they waited for background checks and exit visas, many went from middle class to poor. They had trouble affording food and shelter. Many became sick and weak.

My family kept to a daily food budget. They bought produce at the bazaar and then came back to the rooms to make meals; they rationed the food we ate. No one knew how long we would have to stay in Van, and our money would have to stretch to feed four adults and two children.

As with any group of people kept in a confined space who share language and culture, a society begins to grow. The refugee community in Van became a microcosm for Iranian society. People happily traded gossip, and to pass the long days, many gathered together to share stories about why and how they had come over the border.

My mother said she could pick out the political refugees, because whenever they were pulled into these conversations, their stories were all similarly vague.

~

Van, Turkey, September 2018

The plane was filled with young men, small and wiry with light brown or hazel eyes, who looked Kurdish to me. Many of the women were wearing hijabs wrapped tightly to frame their faces in the Syrian way. I looked out of the window at the dramatic display of lakes and jutting mountains below.

Van, a city filled with Kurds and Turks, had literal busloads of Iranians coming over the mountains from Tabriz and Khoy to shop and holiday. I had read somewhere there were Iranian, Afghan, and Syrian refugees coming over the same mountains we had crossed—close to two hundred people a month. Van was also reportedly a stop on the underground railroad for gay men trying to get out of Iran and into Europe. For so many, Van was a step closer to safety.

In June 2018, the State Department had issued a travel advisory for all Americans going to Turkey, warning them not to go to the country's southeastern border, including the city of Van. "Terrorist attacks, including suicide bombings, ambushes, car bomb detonations, improvised explosive devices, as well as kidnappings for ransom, shootings, roadblocks, and violent demonstrations have occurred in these areas."

It was a level 4, Do Not Travel warning specifically for southeast Turkey, which I decided to flaunt, but carefully: I registered with the State Department and booked myself into a nice hotel. I shared my itinerary with friends and family and checked in with people once a day. I had a procedure in place. All I had to do was be smart and careful.

When I arrived at the hotel, I dropped my bags and ran out the door, ready to walk the two plus miles to Van Castle, where I could have a view of the lake and perhaps see Van's white cats with mismatched eyes that swam in its turquoise waters. The sky was large and bright, against which great puffs of clouds flew, and the wind was so soft, I didn't notice that it pulled all the moisture from my body until my mouth went dry.

I tried to take in the rhythm of the city as I walked along. There was an extraordinary amount of development happening all around. City squares were buffed and landscaped, and the playgrounds were full of children playing, parents talking together as they watched their scuttling kids. Just before the castle, there was a beautiful park where visiting Iranian families were picnicking; the sound of Persian being spoken and the sight of teapots sitting atop burners reminded me of some place that could have been home. The wind blew through the tall poplar trees, shaking the leaves like the gentle shudder of a tambourine just before it stills and quiets—a sound that always, always reminded me of Iran.

I kept walking toward the ruins above Lake Van. Just before I arrived at the castle, four young boys rushed over to meet me at the entrance. One by one they pointed at their chests and told me their ages. The eldest said, "I am FORTY. FOR-TY."

"You are FOURTEEN. FOUR-TEEN," I corrected.

They gestured for me to follow them and took off on the side of the cliff, going up the ruins. I thought about how I was supposed to be careful, and perhaps taking care meant not following four kids through a broken piece of barbed-wire fencing up the rock face of a national tourist site. But then it seemed more fun to follow them, and anyway, one of the boys told me his name was Azad, which means "free," so I followed.

The five of us ran, climbed, and billy-goated our way to the castle walls, which were—it is only now occurring to me—built to keep folks out. From above the walls, a man started yelling and the boys turned to me to say that the tour was over.

"Give me money," they said together, and I handed them fifty liras, the equivalent of about eight dollars. I continued the climb toward the walls but I kept slipping. The rock face seemed to come apart under my hands. Each time I fell, I thought of Mom saying how she'd fallen down the sloped shoulder of the road. I looked toward the mountain range, the one I thought we had climbed over, and wondered how the hell we had made it, weighed down by a pregnant woman, a toddler, an infant, and whatever bags we had.

That night, covered with dust and dirt, I went for an early dinner at the hotel restaurant. The dining room was empty except for a young couple taking selfies as they waited for their food. I looked across the table and I thought about how much my mother would have enjoyed this trip—how many things she'd have to say about it. I remembered her funny way of walking when she was walking fast. Glancing across the table, I thought how she should have been there, sitting across from me.

It happened sometimes: grief hit me broadside and I was toppled. This time highlighted by the absurdity of fate and its fickleness: we walked into this city thirty-six years before and here I was again. That time, we stayed as refugees; now, I was in a beautiful dining room of a multistar hotel.

~

The next day I went to Hotel Kent, the hotel we had limped into that first morning in Van. It had been renovated, but it was still standing. There were still the shoe stalls and the market my mother saw outside her window. It was still favored by Iranians, at least judging by the family I spoke to that was staying there on their holiday. This was the Iranian part of town, only a couple of blocks away from the new developments and buildings popping up in the center of the city, but here were small spice markets and broken sidewalks. This part of town hinted at how Van used to be.

After a half hour of wandering, I found a carpet store that also sold beautiful bags and luggage made from Persian carpets. The salesman spoke a little English; he was an Iraqi Kurd who fled Baghdad after years of working with US forces. He was tired of war and this place was beautiful and relatively peaceful. I told him that I was here because it was the closest I could get to the border between Iran and Turkey.

"It's only an hour to the border," he said. "I can take you there."

"But isn't it dangerous?" I asked.

He looked at me, confused.

"It's OK," he said. "I can take you."

I don't know why, but I said I'd go with him. And we drove out of the city, down the two-lane highway my family had walked on. We stopped along the way so I could say hello to a shepherd and his flock.

All around me was a vast expanse of land reaching to the feet of the mountain range my family had walked over. The peaks were so steep that I can only imagine how perilous they must have been when covered with snow and ice. I saw how remote and shadeless the landscape was. And the place where the smugglers likely abandoned us, the air was so dry, so dry, so dry, I gulped my water and still didn't feel sated. How had we survived without any? There wasn't a streetlight on the highway to the border, not in 1982 and not in 2018.

Before we got to the crossing, the carpet salesman pulled over. I took a picture of the Iranian flag on the border.

"This is the closest I'll get to there," I thought.

He gave me a few minutes before he said, "We should go."

As he turned the car around, I thought about how long it had taken us to walk the same road and now I would be in Van in time for lunch.

On the way back to the city, he told me how this area was a stop for birds as they migrated between North Africa, Iran, and Europe. Twice a year, the lakes were filled with pink and white flamingos—a sight so dramatic and beautiful that he thought he could never leave this place.

TWELVE

Saint Michaels, Maryland, July 2018

Daii and I were eating breakfast on his deck, looking out on the boats bobbing in the water behind his house on the Chesapeake Bay. My uncle had, up until recent months, been largely enthusiastic about my telling this story. But now, years had passed and he'd grown older. Which stories were his to keep and tell, he must have wondered, and which ones was he willing to hand over?

When I interviewed my family and others, especially those who've known me since childhood, I realized I was asking my elders to trust me with their stories and their insights.

They must have thought, *Who are you that I should trust you with this?*

And I remember thinking, *Who are you to keep me from understanding the past?*

I was also thinking, *Who am I to ask you to share your story with me?*

I was also thinking, *Please trust me.*

I was also thinking, *Do I trust you to still love me if I don't see things the same as you? Do I trust you to love me anyway?*

Before I drove down from Brooklyn to see my mother's side of the family, my best friend, Elana, and I came up with a script that was supposed to remind both the interviewer (me) and the interviewee (them) that they should think of me as a professional, someone who was just asking questions. Someone who was removed and curious. I had often found it easiest to be most myself, most engaged and inspired, when the person across from me was a stranger. I thought I should tell my family members that I was recording these conversations. That I had come to use my professional reportorial skills to dig into this story. I had done a version of this speech before, with everyone I had spoken with about this project. I did it with Daii when he and I first sat down together in 2013. Now, in 2018, I started the speech again, reminding him that we could go on and off the record. My uncle balked.

"On a professional level, I wouldn't be doing this with you," he said.

"You wouldn't?" I asked.

"No."

"Why not?"

"It's not something that I want to do with you professionally," he said. "Do you know how many people wanted to interview me regarding Iran?"

"People have wanted to interview you about our family story?"

"No, other things," he said. Then he said, "Go ahead. I'm going to let you talk. Give me your spiel, so I can hear your spiel."

"Give me a second," I told him. "Let me catch up." I took a breath and tried to say it again. I felt the words catching on my tongue and my hands started to shake, so I sat on them.

I started again. "You're asking why I'm interviewing you, since I've already interviewed you. It's because it's been a few years. My understanding and my relationship with this story are different."

"I just don't understand what story you're going to tell," he said.

But my uncle couldn't resist a good story. He couldn't resist telling it and he certainly couldn't resist living through one. For all his bluster, he was softhearted and devoted to his sisters. So he told me his story, the story of how we met.

~

Mexico, United States, and Turkey, 1982

News traveled fast. Daii, who lived in San Diego, rarely spoke to my mother after she and my father left for Iran in 1979—a long-distance phone call was expensive and there was no way to know if the other person would be home. He remembered sending a few cards, but nothing like a letter. Still, Daii learned about my father's arrest right after it happened. He learned, too, that my mother and I were in hiding. He wasn't surprised on either count.

He knew they weren't the same kids he'd marched with in Berkeley, a bullhorn pressed to his lips as he shouted protest slogans, though what chants he led, he had since forgotten.

In the intervening years, my parents had gone further into the movement. They'd stopped speaking to Khaleh, Daii's and my mother's sister, when she accepted the position in the shah's cabinet as the minister of women's affairs. Her husband was also working under the shah. My parents cut them off completely. It must have been especially painful for the sisters—my mother and Khaleh—but it happened. Daii, at that point, was outside of both the political and familial fray. He was caught up in his own life, but he still felt close to my mother and my father.

"Why?" I asked.

"It was the time that we spent together," he said.

~

Daii was hanging out in the pool of the Princess Hotel in Acapulco when he learned we had escaped Iran. The man behind the bar that was built into the hotel pool handed my uncle a bulky first-generation wireless phone.

Khaleh, who was in exile in Washington, DC, was on the other end of the line, telling her brother that my mother and I were in Van and we weren't allowed to leave the city. She was worried, because the baby was due in a few weeks.

Daii said he'd come to get us.

The timing wasn't great. He was meant to start a new job in Dallas in two weeks as the head of Project SEED, a math-focused educational nonprofit working with schools and children in underserved communities. He had secured a $500,000 grant and had a meeting on the calendar with Dallas's superintendent of schools and the president of the Dallas Citizens Council for the week he started. The meeting couldn't be rescheduled, so he had to move quickly. He flew back to San Diego and got through to my mother in Turkey.

Don't come, she said. *You won't be able to do anything.*

He told her it didn't matter. Worst case, they got to spend time together; best case, she'd get out in time to have the baby in the States.

She remembered that he said, *Don't worry. Your family is behind you. You're not alone. We'll do whatever we can to help you.* Which was exactly what she had known he would say.

She wanted to hear that her big brother would come for her and take care of everything.

It was what she needed to hear.

~

My uncle flew from San Diego to Dallas, from Atlanta to New York, and then Germany. As he waited to board the plane for Ankara, Turkey, the flight attendants ushered all the passengers onto the tarmac and searched their luggage. My uncle started speaking with a tall American man, a fellow passenger who was standing near him. They complained about the delay. They talked about sports and their work. The American said he worked for a contractor that manufactured jet fighters, and the company was in the process of selling several planes to the Turkish government. Then, their bags were loaded onto the plane. The two men took their seats.

When the plane landed at the Ankara airport, a military official was standing on the tarmac, rooting through each piece of luggage. He pulled a reel of film from the bag belonging to the tall American. Daii shouted at the official to put it down. Perhaps it was my uncle's tone and gestures, but the official shrugged, handed the film back to the tall American, and let him pass.

Together, Daii and the American made their way through passport control and customs. As the line inched along, my uncle looked over the dirty green walls, trying to get a sense of the city and country he was about to walk out into for the first time. He needed to find a hotel—a nice place with a reliable phone line, where he could figure out a way to get to his little sister.

The tall American said he had a Turkish colleague who might know a place for my uncle to stay. When the Turk arrived to pick up the American, he invited my uncle to stay with them in the company's suites.

When Daii called the US Embassy for help, a staffer brushed him off. They said that my mother and I weren't the first American citizens who fled Iran and were now stuck in Turkey. No, they couldn't do anything.

The American and the Turk suggested my uncle come along with them to a meeting they had scheduled with several retired Turkish generals.

Take five minutes at the start of our presentation, the American said. *Let's see what they can do.*

So the next morning my uncle put on a crisp shirt and suit. He followed the two men into a nondescript hotel conference room and stood opposite a group of strangers dressed in military regalia.

This is a friend, the American said. *He's staying with us and we hope you'll listen to what he has to say.*

Once again, and not for the last time, Daii told the story of his pregnant sister and her daughter, both American citizens who had escaped Iran after his sister's husband was arrested.

I have no idea what to do, my uncle said. *I'm at your mercy.*

One man in full dress uniform said in heavily accented English that while he appreciated my uncle's distress, he couldn't help—none of them could.

Imagine, he said. *Imagine your sister brought heroin or some other drug into Turkey and I helped. My life would be over. My life, my children's lives, and my wife's life. Everything would be over. We can't take this chance.*

That night, the American and the Turk brought Daii with them to an event held at a private club. There, powerful people were milling about, carrying drinks and making conversation. Daii moved through the ornate salons, one room leading to another. He wove his way around the elegantly dressed who were seated at tables where the croupiers flashed cards before pushing and pulling shiny poker chips, the kind a person might see in a Monte Carlo casino. All around him, my uncle knew, money and information were being exchanged.

At the end of the row of rooms, he walked through a set of doors into a courtyard with climbing greenery and flowing fountains. There was a table placed in the center, nearly twenty feet long, and people were seated all around. Waiters were moving around its circumference, bending over to pour wine into glasses.

My uncle took the empty seat next to a gentleman in a dark suit perfectly tailored to his slight frame. The gentleman, Daii remembered, looked like he could have been from anywhere: Europe, the

Mediterranean, or the Near East. He spoke perfect English. He spoke fluent Persian. He told my uncle that he'd once been the Turkish ambassador to some European country but now he was working in the Turkish government. A rapport was established, and the men spoke through much of the evening. And then they said goodbye.

The next morning my uncle went back to the airport to try and book a flight to Van.

~

In the early 1980s, Turkey was under military control. Rule of law was uncertain; the government was preoccupied with the threat of Armenian militants and the reality of guerrilla tactics, which included explosives and other acts of terrorism and resistance. At eight in the morning, my uncle entered the nearly empty international terminal at the Ankara airport. He learned that he couldn't fly into Van—the airport there had been closed for months.

He found a pay phone but none of the Turkish coins he tried to shove into the slot could make it work. Flustered, he picked up his brief-case, threw his bag and camera case over his shoulder, and walked outside the building looking for help when a plainclothes officer and a man in uniform holding a machine gun walked toward him. They ordered him to return to the terminal and guided him through the building's maze of corridors and backrooms before stopping to sift through his luggage. They pulled out his epilepsy medication. They held up the bottle as if the gesture was a question.

Doctor, my uncle said, pointing to the meds.

He pulled out his American passport and pointed to the pills again.

Doctor, he repeated, trying not to let panic and frustration seep into his voice.

Finally, they let him go. Once again, my uncle wove his way through the belly of the terminal to the building's outside.

He found a phone, and a cabbie gave him the tokens to make it work. He called the suites where the American and the Turk were staying. *They're coming through the door now,* the concierge said.

~

The only way for my uncle to get to Van, the Turk said, was to drive there. He told Daii to hire a man called Ilyas, who worked as a driver for the US Embassy. Ilyas couldn't speak English, but he had a car and was about to take a two-week vacation. My uncle was told to hire another man called Abbas, who didn't speak much English either but had once been a reporter and still had an official press pass, which might prove useful.

Then, the Turk had another suggestion: the man my uncle had been seated next to in the garden the night before was the deputy minister of the Turkish secret service.

Might be worth seeing if he can help, the Turk said.

Within hours, my uncle walked into a massive government building and asked for the deputy minister by name and the deputy minister came out to meet him.

He didn't invite Daii into his office, and the warm comradery of the night before was gone, but my uncle pressed on. He had briefly told the deputy minister his story the night before, now he told it again: his pregnant sister had escaped with her toddler and they were being detained.

The deputy minister listened, then called his assistant, asked for a piece of paper, and signed the bottom.

Tell my assistant the exact story you told me, he said. *He'll write it here in Turkish and give it to you.*

I'm late for a meeting, he said, excusing himself.

The assistant quickly ushered my uncle into a small office. Again, my uncle told his story. The assistant wrote it down on the paper above the deputy minister's signature and then applied an official stamp.

Later, when my uncle showed the paper to the Turk, he asked the Turk to whom the letter was addressed. Whom did he need to show this to?

It isn't to anybody, the Turkish colleague said. *It's just your statement that your sister escaped and came into Van and nothing else.*

What good is this? my uncle wondered.

~

While he waited for the driver and the former journalist to meet him, Daii went to the bazaar with the American and the Turk. He bought water, diapers, and food for the baby, presents for his new friends' wives, and a bracelet for himself that he'd eventually give to my brother. Once he finished, the three men went back to their lodging and had a few drinks before finally, close to midnight, a bruised and battered 1964 Chevy pulled up outside the building—metallic blue with deep red panels on the sides.

Sir, don't worry, said Ilyas as he stepped out of the vehicle. *Good car. Good engine.*

Daii handed Abbas, the former reporter, the big, beautiful camera he'd brought with him from the States and Abbas hung it around his neck, trying to embody the image of a journalist on the road.

Daii climbed into the back seat. As they drove out of the city, he looked out of the window and watched the lights of the city fade into the vast darkness of the Turkish countryside.

By dawn, they had gone through half the country and most of the water my uncle had bought. They needed food and rest, so they pulled into a roadside tea house where the seats were made from old tires nailed together.

My uncle was parched. He wanted water but was worried about getting sick, so he ordered tea, thinking it would be safer. He drank one cup of sweet mint tea, then another and another, before he noticed Ilyas had pulled out a handkerchief full of pills. The corners of the fabric were blackened from being tied and untied many times.

Ilyas saw Daii watching him.

Sir, he said, *the tea, sometimes no good.*

~

There were checkpoints on the roads between Ankara and the border. The military junta was looking for terrorists and drug smugglers. At one stop, the guards accused Daii of being an Armenian terrorist. They pulled him and Ilyas from the car and pushed them down on the road, their chin and cheeks pressed into the asphalt. My uncle remembered they drew large automatics, likely machine guns.

My uncle had been drafted into the US Army during the Vietnam War. He was trained for situations like this. The main thing, he knew, was to stay focused and not panic. He calmed himself and stayed so still that the men with the guns wouldn't be tempted to do anything.

Abbas got out of the car, waving his press pass, and then started taking pictures. The guards began to yell but eventually decided to let them go.

My uncle got to his feet. His eyes scanned the horizon for a light in the distance, but there was nothing.

Am I going to be able to get to her? he thought. *Will I get to her in time?*

Then, he thought, his breath catching: *How the hell am I going to get her back home?*

~

It was midday by the time the Chevy rolled into Van. Daii saw a guard standing outside the hotel where we were staying. My uncle didn't know if they were letting people move in and out of the building freely, so he decided to charge into the building and find us.

This was the plan: My uncle and Ilyas would run into the hotel together, with Abbas following and snapping pictures. Then, Daii would slap down his American passport on the reception desk and demand to be let upstairs to our rooms.

Ilyas, Abbas, and my uncle found a place to clean up after their drive. Daii washed his face and shaved. He changed into a clean sports coat and pants and picked up his red leather briefcase.

The three men practiced their roles a few times before they decided to go for it and bounded into the building, with Abbas flashing the camera.

My sister's here, Daii said to the guard. *We're going up.*

~

One moment, my mother remembered, she was crying on the phone with her brother-in-law in the United States; the next the door swung open and her big brother was there. He swept into the room.

It seemed very small and he seemed very big.

His solidity, she said, reassured her. She felt protected.

~

My uncle remembered that he pushed the door open and my mother turned around to look at him. She was wearing a long, black dress with small geometric designs—the same one she had worn when she left Iran. She was crying and smiling at the same time.

He grabbed her and held her.

It's okay, he said. *I'm here.*

And there I was, sitting in the room, watching this reunion—my eyes round and scared.

~

Before my mother left Iran, my grandfather had told her, *The only reason I'm sending my youngest daughter is because* you're *going. I'm putting her in your hands. Wherever you go, take her with you. Don't part from her.*

Now my mother told Daii, *If you want me to come, whatever you arrange for me, you have to arrange for Ameh.*

Through a series of miracles—luck and tenacity—my uncle was able to meet with the head of police and the governor. As the deputy minister's letter landed in front of the right people, the obstacles that blocked us from leaving the city were removed, one by one. My mother, Ameh, and I were allowed to leave Van immediately. It all happened in a day. It seemed like a flash—a wave of paper and we were free.

Amu, Shahrazad, and the baby weren't allowed to come with us, but the authorities told Daii they'd let them go in another month.

~

Ameh felt her stomach fall as we said goodbye to Amu, Shahrazad, and the baby. We didn't know it then, but the authorities lied: it would be many more months before Amu, Shahrazad, and the baby would be able to get visas to go to Spain. From there, they would eventually make it back to California and start their lives again.

But all that was still to come. The afternoon we said goodbye, my mother, Ameh, and I got into the blue Chevy with my uncle. Along the way, we ate and drank whatever was put in front of us. It was a roughly fourteen-hour drive to Ankara, and then a few more hours to Istanbul, where Daii checked us into the Hilton.

We walked into the lobby: Ameh, my mother, and I, each of us caked in a layer of dust and sweat. My mother's dress was torn and frayed at the hem.

And then came Daii; he was dressed beautifully, the very image of casual sophistication.

He booked two rooms.

In the morning at breakfast, Ameh watched as I gripped the spoon and steadily shoveled mounds of honey and cheese into my mouth. I didn't stop to breathe. I ate as if someone would take the food away. I still eat that way sometimes.

~

We quickly learned that Ameh couldn't come with us to the States. The only place the eighteen-year-old could go that didn't need an entry visa was Spain. My mother called a friend for help. This woman's husband had been killed in the Amol insurrection and she was now helping to settle Iranian refugees in Madrid. She said she had room for Ameh, so my mother decided to send her there until plans could be made to bring her to the United States.

Meanwhile, my uncle was trying to get my passport sorted out and find a doctor, approved by an airline, who would sign off on letting my mother fly in the last month of her third trimester. It took time but finally, late one evening, my uncle got a name and address. He bought a bottle of Johnnie Walker Black Label and rang the doctor's doorbell.

The doctor was a thin man, a few years older than Daii, and annoyed that a stranger was coming by so late.

My uncle apologized but explained he needed the doctor's help. The doctor shook his head and started to close the door when my uncle said, *Please. Hear me out.*

He flashed the bottle of Scotch whisky, asked the doctor where he was from, and took a step inside.

Missouri, the doctor replied and stepped aside.

For talkers like my uncle, one detail is all they need to get going. Daii started talking about his time on a riverboat and about the city of Hannibal. The two men started riffing, going on about why Samuel Clemens changed his name to Mark Twain and the rascal Huck Finn. The doctor poured a drink for both of them.

Most Americans in Turkey don't know Missouri, the doctor said.

It took three hours and half a bottle before the doctor wrote the letter that would let my mother get on a plane back to the United States. Another slip of paper that could be so easily lost or torn—it was precious like gold. It meant we could leave Turkey the very next day.

~

My mother was ambivalent about returning to the United States. She didn't want to leave my father far behind. The more space she let come between them, the more it felt as if she were deserting him.

She was also still a leftist revolutionary—the thought of coming back and living in Reagan's America didn't feel right to her. Part of her wanted to stay in Turkey, because at least it was close to Iran. At least she could still hear Iranian radio and read Iranian newspapers—the flavor of the country wouldn't be distant. She was grieving the life she was leaving. A life where she had been happy, one where she felt she had a purpose. But she also had my brother to think about and me; we'd be safer in the United States.

This ambivalence didn't exist for my uncle. He felt equally American and Iranian; the two parts of him didn't thrash against each other. After years of not seeing each other, brother and sister met again with what she felt were diametrically opposed views of the country they were heading toward.

My mother didn't think my uncle could understand her pain over being separated from her husband, whom she loved more than anything else in the world, whose life was in danger, and whose life meant more to her than her own.

My uncle, on the other hand, was terrified. He felt that our safety—our very lives—hinged on his ability to get us out of Turkey and back on US soil.

This is what happens sometimes. People can be inches apart, devoted to each other, and still experience different realities. Like that day when my uncle and mother were standing next to each other at the airport.

This was how my mother told the story to her sister in a recorded interview in 1991:

Mom: I remember we were standing in line at the airport in Istanbul. He was trying to get my ticket for the United States and trying to get Ameh's ticket to send her to Madrid, and he breaks into song. The song that he sings is "Never to see his funny face again, never to be in his embrace again."

He was singing it as if, *This is a pretty song and aren't I singing it well?*

I looked at him, and I said, *How could you possibly sing that song to me now?*

He could not—maybe because Faramarz wasn't there, maybe because the years he hadn't seen him—My life was just in chaos . . . I can't describe it.

This was my uncle's version of the same moment, told to me in 2018:

Daii: I felt pressure because your mom was getting bigger and bigger. She looked like she could give birth any minute. I was always surprised afterward that she made it to California and had some time before she gave birth.

Neda: What happened to Ameh?

Daii: Well, I'd gotten her a ticket to Spain because I could not get her—I tried very hard—but I could not get her to the States. So, okay, at least we'll get her to Spain. The problem was that her passport was very obviously fake. I mean, it wasn't a nice fake, it was fake-fake and if anybody paid close attention to it, they would know.

The first thing we were going to do at the airport was to get her on a plane, and then we'd go about our own business. Once we got to the gate for the guy to check the passport, I started acting like a fool. You know, distracting the guard and, as much as possible, acting like a real American.

Neda: Do you remember at some point you were singing?

Daii: Yeah, I actually had her passport and as I handed it to the guy, I was kidding with him and singing and all kinds of nonsense. You know, you make them laugh. They were laughing a little bit, they stamped her passport, and she got through. Once she got through, I started breathing. You don't know if there is another checkpoint or not, but fortunately she got through that one. We waited until her plane took off, so now we could breathe a sigh of relief.

Neda: What was that like for her? Did she and I say goodbye?

Daii: She hugged you and she kissed you.

Neda: She was my person.

Daii: She was the person who was principally taking care of you while we were . . . around everything. You know?

～

Two days later, my uncle, my mother, and I landed at Dulles International Airport just outside Washington, DC. When we got off the plane, Daii knelt down and kissed the ground.

Inside the terminal, Khaleh's husband, Reza, saw us first. He hadn't seen my mother in many years, but when he saw me he picked me up and held me close. As we walked together through the airport, I saw a stuffed Pink Panther in a gift shop window.

Very seriously I told my uncle Reza that I didn't have a Pink Panther and he bought it for me. It was nearly my size and I could barely carry it so I pulled it along behind me as we walked to meet Khaleh and my grandmother.

～

"So, that's your story," Daii said.

It was night in Saint Michaels and we both had a drink in front of us.

I smiled at him.

"Thanks for coming to get us, D," I said.

～

That first night in Washington we went to Khaleh and Reza's house. It was the first time in eight years that the whole of my mother's family was together. Before the Iranian Revolution in 1979, my mother felt she and Khaleh and Reza were completely opposed in every way. Khaleh and Reza were monarchists—my aunt was the minister of women's affairs and eventually my uncle would be the shah's biographer.

Now, they were all together again. And in many ways, it was almost as if they hadn't been apart, though there was lingering tension on both sides: My mother still despised the shah's regime, while her sister and brother-in-law believed she'd betrayed the progress they had worked so hard to achieve. There were topics, mostly politics, that the family members couldn't talk about without enormous fights breaking out.

But somehow their friendship and the deep love were still there.

~

One day a few months before she died, my mother told my brother a story. When I was about two years old, she took me with her to visit her father in Kerman. While we were there, my mother and I went to a party held at her cousin's manor.

The party was outside on the lawn of the old, majestic building made of stone and brick. Connecting the two wings of the house was a long outdoor passage lined with arches and columns. I was in one room, play-ing with the servant's son. My mother and her cousin were standing at opposite ends of the outdoor walkway, talking to each other. My mother was holding on to her cousin's son's hand. He was just a little older than me. He let go of my mother's hand and ran into the house. Just then, the ground began to move. It rolled hard beneath my mother's feet.

Earthquake, my mother's cousin cried.

She screamed at my mother to jump out from under the covered passage. My mother did and fell into a rose bush. The thorns tore at her skin. She looked up at the house and watched as the roof broke apart and came together like teeth gnashing.

All at once, my mother remembered me, and started to scream. She tried to drag herself toward the house, but the ground was moving too hard and she couldn't get to her feet. I was dead, my mother was sure I was dead.

Everything quieted.

My mother screamed my name. Someone called out, *I have her!*

Someone else called out that my mother's cousin's son was safe. And then the ground began to pitch again. My mother held on to the ground and watched the ancient house buck and shake. Then, it stilled.

Later that night, my mother and I returned to my grandfather's house. It had been badly damaged. When my mother went to the room where I was staying, she saw that the ceiling had collapsed on top of my bed.

If the earthquake had struck another night, I would have been dead.

I know about luck, my mother said. *I've had good luck and I've had bad luck. I've had them both.*

THIRTEEN

Monterey Peninsula, California, 1982

Back in the States, my mother followed her mother back to the beautiful town by the Pacific Ocean that she said felt like death to her. This started what was—up until that point—the hardest period in her life.

My mother immediately enrolled me in preschool. I didn't speak English, but she didn't have the patience to sit with me every day. She and my grandmother thought I'd learn the language more quickly and acclimate to life in the United States faster by going to school than by being with my mother at home.

For three weeks before my brother, Nema, was born, Mom would call Iran every day and speak to my father's older brother. The family didn't know how things would unfold for my father and the others who had been arrested. They knew only that the government normally kept political prisoners for about six months before they killed them. My mother prayed for a coup. If there was a coup, then maybe my father and the others would be released.

But then the rumors started about people being able to bribe guards, interrogators, and mullahs to get their loved ones out of Evin. The rumors seemed to gain strength after the names of several people who'd been arrested with my father weren't read over the radio with the others. Later, we learned that their names hadn't been read because they were already dead, killed by torture within days of their arrest.

But whispers were flying that people with money who knew people in influential positions could arrange for the prisoners to escape. Then, the released would sort of dissolve back into society.

My father's family started trying to find some way to save him. Someone tried to make contact with the mullahs, interrogators, and guards working in Evin. A contact asked for millions of tomans to get my father out. Ours wasn't the only family trying to get a loved one released; there were several.

My mother started asking friends and family in the United States for money. She asked Khaleh and Reza, Rostam, my father's childhood friend, and others. Old friends and family gave money to help get my father out, sometimes thousands of dollars, even though they knew it would likely come to nothing. My father's parents had money they had saved with Rostam in New York, and they had it sent back to them in Iran.

The plan was to bribe someone to get him out or to get his sentence reduced. It was a foolish plan, perhaps, but my mother thought that even if there were just a 1 percent chance that it might work, she would rather grab at that chance than do nothing at all. Someone must have made a lot of money fleecing desperate people like us.

Around this time, at the end of September 1982, my brother was born. It wasn't too long afterward that the families of the prisoners were finally allowed to visit.

My mother was told that while the prisoners were pale, thin, and tired, they seemed to be okay. None showed obvious signs of torture, and many seemed to still have hope. But perhaps they didn't, perhaps they had been told how to behave, or maybe they were just trying to be brave.

After that first visit, the prison allowed the families to come every month. My mother would sit by the phone in my grandmother's hallway in Monterey and wait for any news about Dad or their friends.

Where there's a dearth of real information, into that void comes gossip and hearsay. A story spread that my mother and father talked while he was in prison. Another that she was able to call him and give him the news that my brother had been born. People suggested my parents had privileges they didn't. These weren't the only falsehoods; there were many together that fomented division among those who were in exile, in hiding, far away, and afraid.

My mother's days while she waited to hear what would happen to my father went like this: she took me to school; she took care of a newborn; she went swimming; and she wrote long letters to my father's family in Iran.

She tried to make dinner every night and make sure the house wasn't a mess before my grandmother came home from work, but an adult child moving home after so many years away can be hard under any circumstances.

My grandmother was jealous of my mother's relationship with my father's family and was annoyed that now my mother was back at home, she was preoccupied with speaking to them and hearing from them.

My mother for her part resented being back in Monterey. She hated feeling powerless and rudderless. She couldn't find a job or go to school until she knew what happened to my father. It was the Reagan era; she had only been away for four years, but in that time, it seemed like the United States had changed a great deal.

The yuppies had replaced the hippies and revolutionaries; there was a kind of affluence she hadn't seen before, particularly in Monterey. Even her own mother had moved into a beautiful townhouse, decorated beautifully. She wondered if everyone had become rich in the years since she had left. She didn't see her politics reflected anywhere.

My grandmother, like Daii, loved the United States; like her son, she felt at home in America. She thought my mother's views dishonest, and maybe a bit hypocritical.

My mother, on the other hand, was preoccupied with trying to find a way to go back to Iran. She tried to make sure I didn't forget my Persian. She bought me Iranian storybooks and played Iranian music and tried to stay as removed from life in the United States as she could.

She'd feel hopeful when my uncle Farid would call to say they'd given money to a mullah at Evin, and he'd promised that he was going to check with my father's interrogator.

Then her hopes would rise again when he'd call the next day and say that the interrogator said that my father would be released soon.

For two straight weeks, my uncle and mother would talk on the phone every day, telling each other that the next day my father would be released.

One time, she remembers that Farid called and said, *God willing, by next Friday I'll have your husband at the border, and you may have him back in a week.*

She started to believe my father might come home, then my uncle would call again and say that something unforeseen had happened. The bribes went nowhere, and the mullahs and the interrogators would say enough for my uncle not to lose hope and for my mother to keep going. As long as she could try to save him, she didn't feel completely helpless.

She had a newborn and a toddler, and a long-shot scheme to have her husband smuggled out of prison. The days passed until the mother of two of the men who were in prison with my father called to say that their trial had started.

My mother spoke to my father's sister, Minna, in Tehran. The morning papers had just been published, and they had printed the charges against my father. The prosecution was asking for the death penalty.

One by one, my aunt read the names of the prisoners and the charges against them, which included working for the CIA and against the Islamic Republic.

All the things my mother had started to believe were wrong.

~

The trial started just after the January New Year 1983. Every day my mother would wake up and take me to preschool. Then, she'd go back home and sit on the floor with her back against the wall and wait. She would call Tehran three or four times a day to get the latest news.

The proceedings weren't held in a courthouse but in the auditorium in Evin. There was a stage with the mullahs and prosecutors sitting on one side and twenty-five prisoners, sitting in rows, on the other.

In front of the stage, hundreds of people from Amol who had lost a loved one in the uprising were sitting crossed-legged on the floor. The space was decorated with banners condemning the prisoners as a giant portrait of Khomeini looked on. The audience was encouraged to call out for the prisoners' deaths.

There wasn't a defense counsel. Each of the accused had to try and defend themselves. The whole thing was broadcast every evening across state television.

~

Evin Prison, Tehran, January 1983

In the name of God, the merciful. Your honor, the Revolutionary Court of the Islamic Republic of Iran. I present you the indictment against the accused, Mr. Faramarz Toloui-Semnani. Married. Born: 1944. Lives in Tehran. He's a central member of the Union of Iranian Communists. Religion: Communism. Arrested: July 1982. Charges are as follows:

1. Central and leading member of the Union of Iranian Communists.
2. Participated in the organization's conferences in order to establish the general policies for taking up arms against

the government of the Islamic Republic of Iran.

3. Member of Tehran committee of the Union of Iranian Communists and was in contact with Marxist members of factories.

4. Permanent member of the Union of Iranian Communists, in charge of internal communications throughout Iran.

5. Contact for the chief financial officer for the Union of Iranian Communists, in order to transfer almost 8 million rials from the southern branch of the Union of Iranian Communists to the central branch. The money stolen by this organization from the Keshavarzi Bank of Khuzestan was meant to be loaned to the respectable people of that city.

6. Representative for the Union of Iranian Communists at the Confederation's conference whose main goal was creating a unified Communist Party in order to fight the Islamic Republic of Iran.

The accused, Faramarz Toloui, is an experienced Communist and is one of the organization's longest-serving members. He was once even the secretary general of the Union of Iranian Communists, and played a special role during his fifteen-year stay in America by corrupting the youth of Iran.

After the revolution, he returned to the country and, until his arrest, held leadership positions in the heathen organization, Union of Iranian Communists or what they call "Sarbedaran-e Jangal."

Given this information, and his active and sensitive role in the organization, it is clear to the court of the Islamic Republic that he's guilty. I'm asking for the highest punishment.

Prosecutor for the Islamic Republic of Iran
Sayyed Asadollah Lajevardi

TRIAL OF FARAMARZ TOLOUI-SEMNANI[12]

Judge Ayatollah Gilani: Mr. Toloui, the prosecutor just read your public indictment. Do you agree with Article 1: "Central and leading member of the Union of Iranian Communists"?

Faramarz Toloui-Semnani: Yes, from March 1979 until the organization changed direction to become the Sarbedaran-e Jangal.

Judge: Second charge: "Participated in the organization's conferences in order to establish the general policies for taking up arms against the government of the Islamic Republic of Iran."

Toloui-Semnani: That's not correct. The UIC didn't have conferences. It had councils. It's right that I participated in three of them, but not to plan to overthrow the Islamic Republic. The first council was held in March '77 or '78, and it was held outside of Iran. This was before the revolution, so naturally, it couldn't have been against the Islamic regime.

The second council was held in March '79, a week before the referendum. In volume 27 of the journal *Haghighat*—I believe your honor has a copy—there were three points in defense of the revolution. Of course, at that time the Union of Iranian Communists did not believe in an *Islamic* revolution, but it did believe in defending the revolution and the leadership of the revolution against the US and Soviet powers. The council also felt our duty was to criticize the interim government— by that I mean, to criticize wrongdoings and praise good work.

Then, the third council, which took place in March 1980, was to prepare for a possible American coup. There are available minutes of the

---

12 I had the charges against my father and his testimony translated from the government's transcripts. They have been edited for length and clarity.

Third Council that show we endorsed the leadership of the revolution and [Ayatollah Khomeini] the Imam of the Nation. We supported the Islamic Republic and supported the occupation of the US Embassy. All of these were agreed to and later published in a newsletter that was publicly distributed. I'm sure your honor has copies.

Judge: So, you're saying you don't agree to the charge because it wasn't a "conference" but a council and the agenda wasn't against the Islamic Republic.

Toloui-Semnani: No.

Judge: Do you mean it wasn't on the agenda, to topple the Islamic government? Is this the gist of your answer?

Toloui-Semnani: I am pointing to the introduction Mr. Prosecutor read this morning, if you remember correctly, that in January 1981, or June 1980, the Union's agenda—at least officially and on paper—was not to take up arms against the Islamic Republic.

At the third council, it was decided that we should be ready to defend the revolution and the Islamic Republic against a possible imperialist American attack.

Judge: The third article charges that members of the Tehran chapter of the organization were in contact with Marxist members working in pharmaceutical, shoes, and sweets factories. What do you say about this?

Toloui-Semnani: I participated in the Tehran committee of the Union of Iranian Communists from December 1981 to March 1982 but not as an official member. I was allowed to participate under the condition that I wouldn't promote my stance against the Sarbedaran Movement. I was in contact with three members of the Tehran committee—actually two—all of whom were arrested and are present here.

Judge: To summarize, your answer to the third article of the indictment is that you were not a member of the Tehran Committee. Is that what you are saying?

Toloui-Semnani: I was not. From December to March 1982, I was just a person who went to meetings and my contacts were not Communists working in the factories. I was in contact with members of the Union of Iranian Communists who were in touch with people who worked in those factories.

Judge: Very well. The fourth article, "Permanent member of the Union of Iranian Communists, in charge of internal communications throughout Iran." What do you say to that?

Toloui-Semnani: After the third council until the plan for the Sarbedaran Movement was approved, I was a member of the Permanent Committee. From approximately one month after the start of the Iran-Iraq War to June 20, 1981, I was in charge of communication between the provinces and the central committee in Tehran. However, when the group changed its mission, I left the Permanent Committee in protest. The organization wanted me to go to the jungle and help lead the Sarbedaran movement, but I did not go.

Judge: Fifth article: "Contact for the chief financial officer of the organization in order to ensure that almost eight million rials in cash were moved from the southern provinces to the treasury." What do you have to say about this charge?

Toloui-Semnani: I was in contact with the chief financial officer up until the point where the organization changed its agenda.

A man who's here now gave me six hundred or eight hundred tomans to give to the organization. Also at this time, a box was given to me to deliver to the finance chief. I have no information as to how this money was attained or whether it was related to what the indictment says. This is written in all my interrogations, as well.

Judge: Yes . . . the interrogator accused most of you of having connections with the CIA. What do you have to say about that?

Toloui-Semnani: To answer this question, I need to speak in a bit more detail about the time I spent abroad. Would you allow me?

Judge: How many years were you abroad?

Toloui-Semnani: I was abroad almost fifteen years. I was almost eighteen years old when I left, and I went to America to become an engineer and then return to Iran as soon as possible. I thought that being specialized could free me from imperialism. After some reflection, I realized this was a fantasy.

A regime like the much-hated Pahlavi regime depends on Western imperialism. It's conservative and its hands are dirty with the blood of the people. My so-called academic expertise cannot make a difference in this ocean of misery. I almost returned [to Iran] when I was done with my master's degree, but after speaking with others, I realized we must fight against the monarchy. I came to this conclusion. I made the choice to discover my own destiny and try to save others.

Let me try to explain: When I left Iran, I didn't understand Islam—

Judge: What did your father do?

Toloui-Semnani: My father worked in import-exports.

I learned Islam in the typical Quran and Sharia classes taught in those times. When we were abroad, and we decided to do something [against the shah], we tried to find our way but our options were limited. One was an organization called the Confederation and the other was the Muslim student association in America and Canada.

When I looked into the association of Muslim students, I found that it was completely connected to Saudi Arabia; the kingdom even paid for their tuition, airfare, and travel.

But the Confederation didn't seem to have a specific ideology: It defended Shiites and political prisoners. Its members were both Marxist and non-Marxist, those who believed in Islam and Christianity. It was a democratic organization, so it didn't belong to any ideology, except to fight against the shah.

We had no choice but to gravitate toward the Confederation because there really was no other movement to join. It was during the height of the Vietnam War, and by the time the Vietnam War ended two years after I joined the movement, the majority of the Confederation leaned communist. It was the influence of the Vietnam War protests and the fact that revolutionary Muslims didn't seem to have a solution.

The Confederation was never dependent on any foreign government. Before the revolution and after, there were many attempts to find documents against the Confederation, or at least the shah wanted someone to find evidence that it was foreign funded, because the movement caused him so much trouble abroad. There wasn't any proof of foreign interference in the Confederation.

The Confederation didn't let us push ideology. I was active in the Confederation and was never allowed to push Marxist ideology. In later years, I was Marxist—most were—we saw no other way, no other path to a solution.

The Confederation depended on its student members to fund it through their own money. When we sent lawyers to Iran to help with the trials, it was done with the students' money.

The truth is that we lived for a few years in the heart of American imperialism. We learned its dirty ways and witnessed its politics and schemes. And from all of this we learned one thing, that an organization of a few thousand students could not be dependent on any government.

Finally, let me add this, the Union of Iranian Communists whose name the prosecutor mentioned was directly responsible for organizing the 1977 protest in Washington. It was there that the shah and his master [President] Carter cried. Maybe the film was shown in Iran, too. Carter wrote about it in his memoir, about what the Iranian students did to him, and how they made him cry.

Carter planned to put almost two thousand people—six hundred of whom were SAVAK agents—in front of the White House and the television news was supposed to show them as the supporters of the Pahlavi regime. At the same time, Iranian students from different parts of the Confederation, including the Union of Iranian Communists which I was part of, gathered at a corner of the White House on the grass.

On the day of the protest, we dressed fifty of our own people to look like US government officials. Then, we armed almost twenty-five hundred students with sticks. When the shah arrived, the military was supposed to do the twenty-one-gun salute as a sign of respect. After the seventh shot, our plan was to attack the area where the SAVAK agents were seated.

We attacked them with our sticks and shields. The police confronted us, and we fought back, sending ninety SAVAK agents and twenty-four police officers to the hospital.

Police then shot tear gas toward the protesters but fortunately the wind was blowing toward the White House, and like a cloud, the gas went inside the White House, affecting almost two hundred people, including police and journalists. There was a big banner that said, "Shah Welcome," and the students tore it up in front of the news cameras.

I remember after this victory the Imam of the Nation thanked the Iranian students. I don't know the exact quote but he said the protest helped clear the path for the Islamic Revolution.

Obviously, our organization wasn't connected to the CIA.

Some of the people on trial today were in charge of the protest. It's obvious that we could not be connected to the CIA, because we weren't working for the United States. This protest took place at least one month before the Qom uprising, when all of the Confederation's leadership, including myself, went into hiding in the States.

Prosecutor Lajevardi: Please say how many days you were in the jungle.

Toloui-Semnani: If I remember right, it was one day and two nights in the month of August or September, 1981. I was there one or two weeks after the group went into the jungle.

Prosecutor: Did you go to convince them to stop? How come you went there if you didn't believe in their mission?

Toloui-Semnani: Please allow me—if the respected Judge Ayatollah Gilani permits me, I'll explain. On June 20, the Union of Iranian Communists' mission changed. Up to that point, the organization tried its best to support the troops in the Iran-Iraq War. Then, it began questioning things.

The idea of an uprising was suggested at a meeting and from the time it was raised, I was against it for three reasons: First, we agreed to support the Islamic Republic, and an uprising meant we opposed it. Later, myself and the others on trial today realized that there were deep disagreements about this plan. All the leaders—those in charge of central committees and provinces—decided to get together and find a solution.

When we did, there was a vote that an immediate uprising should take place in Tehran. Many leaders opposed this plan, myself included. It was decided that there would be another vote.

Over the next two weeks several friends and I traveled to different provinces to try to explain why we thought an uprising was wrong. It was eventually put to vote, and something like forty-five to forty-six percent of the organization was against the uprising, and fifty-four to fifty-five percent were for it. Those who wanted an uprising didn't think it would be possible to have it in Tehran so they decided to move it to the jungle outside of Amol.

The committee—the one where I was a member—was to lead the uprising. I wouldn't be a part of it but others said that since it was decided, it must be done.

The last time a group was sent to the jungle, they sent me a message that I must go, too. Then, one night they came. They blindfolded me and took me. I stayed two nights. They insisted that I had to be a part of the movement, but I refused.

They said I was going against the rules, and in the next council they'd decide what to do with me. I waited for them to take me back to Tehran, and they did.

I was against the plan because I believed it was wrong.

There are people here among the accused that I spoke to about this. I had neither a provisional role nor a supporting role in the uprising, nor did I try to justify it. I always feared that this would do real damage to people and the Islamic Republic.

Prosecutor: What was your reason?

Toloui-Semnani: I did not believe in an uprising against the Islamic Republic. Never.

Prosecutor: You didn't. You recognized it as an opposition, right?

Toloui-Semnani: As I said, first and foremost, I believed it was against the leadership of the Imam Khomeini, because we had decided to support the leadership of the Islamic Revolution, meaning support the Imam of the Nation.

Prosecutor: There is a saying that a liar has a bad memory.

[Here he quotes the magazine *Haghighat*, which criticizes a central pillar of the Islamic Republic, the *velayat-e faqhih*, the principle that clerics should rule over the state.]
Isn't *Haghighat* yours?

Toloui-Semnani: Yes, it is.

Prosecutor: The organization believed in Imam's leadership?

Toloui-Semnani: There's no doubt that the Confederation was against *velayat-e faqhih*, there is no doubt about that.

Prosecutor: The greatest tenant of the nation's Imam is his belief that the clergy should rule over the state. Basically, if there were only one thing in our religion and in our republic that's important, it would be this.

So, how is it possible that you are against what Imam recognizes as the core of the Islamic Republic, but you're not against him, personally? Did you only like the Imam's skin and his bones or did you like his way of thinking?

Toloui-Semnani: There is no doubt that Imam is the living expression of *velayat-e faqhih*.

In those days, we were saying that we had to follow the Imam because he was an anti-imperialist and an anti-shah leader. Yet, we were against some things he believed in, including the *velayat-e faqhih*.

We believed that we must support any attempt against American imperialism and for Iran's freedom, but when it came to the country's constitution, we were critical of this. But the organization was never against the leaders of the revolution. In the *Haghighat*, there are articles in support of the Islamic Republic, in support of the war and the hostage crisis.

Prosecutor: Gentlemen are now claiming to be the defenders of the revolution and Muslim people and saying that they didn't believe in taking up arms against the Islamic Republic.

How could you say you believed in the Iranian Revolution? How could you stand in front of the court and deny that you didn't believe in armed struggle?

If you were against the uprising in the jungle, you would've come to the authorities and reported it. Despite all that, and until getting arrested, you worked for this organization.

If you were against the uprising, why didn't you report it? What kind of opposition is this? If you were against it, and if you say you accept Imam as the leader of the nation, and if you say you believe in the Islamic Revolution, should you have kept your association with this organization? Shouldn't you have reported it?

Toloui-Semnani: Would you allow me?

Judge: If you have a defense, please say it.

Toloui-Semnani: Would you please allow me to say a few words about the protests that took place in America? I was merely clarifying whether there were connections to the CIA or not—

Prosecutor: Mr. Toloui, this protest of a few intellectuals, of kids abroad, is a nothing protest. It has no value. You had to have something to convince our poor, innocent young people who traveled to Europe and America to throw tomatoes. Shouting a few chants is not a big deal.

You lived in the heart of American imperialism for fifteen years and didn't have the courage to say a word to the American police, and then you dare to come to Iran and try to pierce the heart of the nation of Allah.

You had to throw a few tomatoes; otherwise our children would have never joined you. What you did there was deceive the public.

How did you fight against imperialism? You were raised in the bosom of American imperialism. For fifteen years you sucked its blood. You grew up in America. You didn't even have the courage to slap an American cop across the face.

If you were a man, you would've done this in America, not Iran.

Did you terrorize anyone in America? Why didn't you? Why didn't you have the courage? Why didn't you come to Iran during the shah's reign and commit such crimes? Is it that the Islamic Republic makes it easy to come here, to import guns, to purchase guns in Kurdistan, to steal arms from the front, to attack the lives of people? Are you fighting against imperialism?

Enough is enough.

Your protest in America was an American plot, too. It helped the CIA to make it easier for people like you to recruit the youth.

We believe that you are all supporters of imperialist America; if you weren't, why else would you fight against this nation?

The crowd cheers and chants, "The Nation of Allah fights, dies but doesn't surrender."

Prosecutor: According to the interrogator, Mr. Toloui is a fanatic who refuses to tell the truth. During his interrogation, despite being talked to kindly, he hasn't given any useful information.

He thinks that he's a revolutionary, according to Marxist ideology.

The crowd chants, "A Communist's ally must be executed."

Prosecutor: Even though he has not given us any information, his crimes are so vast that even if he were executed a thousand times, it would not be enough.

That's why our interrogations weren't really about getting any information out of this corrupt man. Such people should not exist in Iran so that the Islamic Revolution can continue.

The crowd chants, "Allah-o-Akbar."

Judge Ayatollah Gilani to Prosecutor Lajevardi: Do you have anything else for him?

Mr. Toloui, please go. You have no other logical defense.

Toloui-Semnani: Please allow me, a few words—

The crowd chants, "Down with Communism."

Judge: This is not a defense. Since you opened your mouth to defend yourself, you have been bringing excuses for yourself.

Lying and scheming have covered your soul. If a human being does something wrong, at least he should tell the truth.

On the one hand you say you were the supporter of the Imam. However, this *Haghighat* magazine reveals you're lying right away. The prosecutor held it in front of the cameras so people could see what kind of person we're dealing with.

If you have a logical and reasonable explanation, the court will hear it. Think about it. Fight with your ego to tell the truth.

Toloui-Semnani: First of all, I am not a Marxist anymore. It is true that I was for eight years.

Judge: And after the prison had the pleasure of hosting you, you changed your mind?

Toloui-Semnani: I changed my mind before my arrest. I had serious questions over what Marxists had done around the world, especially in Cambodia and Afghanistan. Why were there so many mass killings and crimes? I was worried about what the Marxists would do, especially after Amol. These were questions I had, concerns I had . . . though in truth most of my thinking took place in the prison.

Prosecutor: These Marxist men, in order to achieve their goals, accept anything but religion. Marxists think that religion is the most decadent thing ever. That's their thinking. These gentlemen in order to achieve their goals are even willing to lie, because they think that our court can be deceived.

We don't care that you've become religious—God willing, it will be for your own good. But we conclude that these Marxists will feign religion, in order to achieve their goals. It's as clear as day.

Toloui-Semnani: Would you allow me to speak, please?

Judge: Think for a while, Mr. Toloui. Please leave now.

Toloui-Semnani: I wasn't lying. What I said about Amol was the absolute truth and the interrogator knows it, as well.

Judge: Very well, you said what you wanted to say. We'll find out what the court thinks of your case.

Toloui-Semnani: So, you'll allow me to speak later?

Judge: You didn't have any reasoning in your defense. If the court gives you another chance, it would only be a bonus and not your right. If you have anything more to say now, please do.

Toloui-Semnani: The organization hurt the Islamic Republic, and the people of Amol. Even though I was not part of it, as God is my witness, I tried everything to stop it and the others here today can testify to that.

I'm not saying this to exonerate myself. I agree with what the prosecutor said: even though the Confederation defended the war and the takeover of the Embassy, that alone doesn't mean anything.

The organization *did* support the revolution, but when the situation in Iran became complicated, in order to find a solution, the means felt justified.

What I said about leaving Marxism is true. It wasn't to exonerate myself, because I'll be considered guilty or innocent depending on what I did while in the organization. I left because I asked myself how we could justify actions that went against our beliefs.

I only hope that God forgives me. I don't say this to exonerate myself in the court. I bow to the families of Amol's martyrs, and I know we can't make up for the damage this did, and I'm glad it was stopped.

Judge: You chose your punishment when you chose Sarbedaran—*head in gallows*—as the name of your organization. Your explanations won't satisfy the people of this nation.

The damage you've done isn't ultimately a big deal. It's just made us stronger. The people of the nation have become stronger.

He who repents, the Great God is forgiving and forgives.

The crowd chants, "Allah-o-Akbar."

∼

There were banners calling for the prisoners' deaths. The audience at the trial was chanting for their deaths. The people reading the charges, who were supposed to be objective, condemned the prisoners.

The prosecutor asked the prisoners to explain and defend themselves.

My mother was told that in the months leading up to and even during the trial, many of the defendants tried to appease the prosecution. In an effort, perhaps, to receive leniency some conceded ground to the regime. They asked for forgiveness; a few said that they acted as agents of the CIA, and some gave detailed information about specific people. Some said they deserved whatever punishment would be doled out to them, including death.

Even though my mother knew all the prisoners were kept in solitary confinement or two to a cell, she was struck by how similar their words sounded. It was as if they had all decided to say the same thing. My mother wondered if maybe the government had promised them a way out.

The news coverage of the trial in the United States suggested that, perhaps, because there was a legal process at all, the Islamic Republic was starting to move in a more moderate direction. The trial lasted two weeks. My mother called her sister in Washington to see if she could come there to wait for the verdict.

I stayed behind with my grandmother.

~

Eastern Shore, Maryland, January 2015

When I began reporting and researching this story, someone gave me a book compiled and published by the Iranian government about the Amol uprising and the subsequent trial. Someone—I don't know who—had smuggled the volume out of the country and it was passed along until it reached me.

Earlier, while my mother was dying, someone had told her about the same book, and she'd asked those who had access to it to read sections to her. Everyone she asked to read it to her refused.

When I got the book, I had sections of it translated. The official account is surprisingly detailed. It seems selectively accurate—some sections are vague or simply wrong; details, names, and events are brushed over or missing. The government does not explain how its evidence was collected, or the circumstances surrounding the arrests, or the methods of interrogation. But there is an apparently thorough account of the uprising, and crucially there is a transcript of the trial.

One cold winter morning in 2015, I sat down to read the trial transcript for the first time. When I finished, I felt at once filled up and depleted. I went for a drive and I found myself in Walmart, holding a loaf of bread, crying in the oatmeal aisle, and talking on the phone to my best friend, Elana.

I thought I was over this, I said. *I thought I was done feeling this.*

Neda, she said, *this is the first time you've heard your father try to explain what happened in his own words.*

It's just— I groped for the right words. *He never had a chance and she thought he did.*

~

Washington, DC, January 1983

The day of my father's sentencing, January 24, coincided with the lead-up to Super Bowl XVII. For the first time in the franchise's history, the Washington Football Team was playing in the championship game. The city had worked itself into a fervor; the streets were decorated in team colors, with red and gold balloons tied to row-house stoops. My mother and her sister went to lunch at a restaurant in DC's Georgetown neighborhood. While they talked about my father and the others who were also waiting for their fate to be decided, the lunch crowd talked excitedly about Sunday's game.

If the Islamic Republic was going to execute my father and the others, my mother believed that they would do it on January 25, the anniversary of the Amol uprising. If the group could survive until Sunday, January 30, it was likely they'd be spared. Years later, in the recorded interview with her sister, she said, "The one thing that is very difficult to explain are the feelings and the thoughts that go through your mind while you're waiting, all the thoughts that go through your mind. There is grief and fear—I can't describe the terror or the anxiety."

That day, however, in a restaurant buzzing with conversation and decorated in red and gold, my mother let herself believe, just for a moment, that the badness might pass us by.

That night she and her sister watched ABC's *Nightline*, which was airing a long story about Iran after the revolution. They showed scenes of crowded Tehran streets and the bustling Grand Bazaar. Then, very briefly, there was a shot of my father hunched over in the front row of the defendants' area in the courtroom. He was surrounded by his comrades and fellow prisoners, a giant poster of the Ayatollah Khomeini high above their heads. The trial was being broadcast daily on state television, and the reporter wondered if this transparency suggested the government was moving toward a more accountable system of law. That brief clip was the first time my mother had seen her husband since the morning of his arrest.

My mother slept that night and woke at dawn. Realizing how early it was, she went back to sleep and dreamed. She dreamed she was standing by a dry riverbed, the kind she said was often found in Iran. It was wide with a rocky bottom. My father was there and he looked happy. In the dream, my mother said to my father: *I think the danger has passed, don't you?*

He didn't say anything, but he was calm, so she began to relax. Then she saw a friend who had stood trial with my father. The expression on his face frightened her.

The danger has passed, hasn't it? she asked this friend, wanting to be reassured. The friend didn't reply. My mother began to panic. She looked at my father.

You said the danger passed, she said. She looked back toward her friend. *Tell me,* she begged them. *Tell me what's happening.*

Her friend avoided her eyes. Then my mother saw one of the organizers of the Amol uprising standing behind my father. It was then she knew they had all been killed.

She woke up then.

It was a dream, she thought, *and dreams don't mean anything.*

~

The telephone rang after breakfast on January 25 and my uncle Reza answered, stayed quiet, and then replaced the receiver. He then walked into the room where my mother was sitting, nursing my brother, and said he had to go out but would be back soon. Forty-five minutes later, my mother heard the door open and saw Khaleh walking up the stairs.

What's wrong? my mother said. *Why are you crying?*

She thought, for some reason, something had happened to someone else. She searched her sister's face and realized she was crying for her and for my father.

They killed him, my mother said, her voice rising to a scream.

~

Washington, DC, July 2018

"What a shame," Khaleh remembered my mother saying as she rocked back and forth. "What a shame, what a shame, what a shame."

When Khaleh told me this, I tried to remind myself I was listening to a story from almost four decades' remove. But then, in my mind, I could see my mother so clearly. I could hear her.

"What a shame," I could hear my mother say in her voice. "Oh, what a shame."

I began to cry. My aunt reached across to hold me.

"This is so hard," she said, crying with me.

~

Evin Prison, Tehran, January 1983

In the Name of God

Today, January 24, 1983, I, Faramarz Toloui-Semnani, received my death sentence, and as my last writing, I am writing a few lines to my relatives, my kind parents, my dear wife, my small and beautiful children, Neda and Nema, and other acquaintances and friends.

Anyone who chooses to walk a certain path must accept all its consequences. First, his intention is important, and people must partially judge him on that. Then, it is his actions that must be the basis for others to remember and to evaluate him. I, too, must be judged based on these two things.

I stepped into this path and did everything with a sacred intention at heart, yet I make no claim on its success, except that I was part of it. I wanted nothing but the complete freedom and independence of Iran. I acted not to betray but to serve my country. You also know I was against the uprising in Amol and opposed to it, but as a member of the organization, I have to accept the consequences and I have. I deeply apologize for putting you through this and ask God to grant you strength and patience since I'll be freed, and the sorrow is left to you.

Mother and Father, please know that I received nothing but love and kindness from you which I can never forget. I only seek your forgiveness.

My dear Farah, my loyal wife, please know that I spent many happy and fruitful years with you. What

I got from you has been kindness, love, and pleasure. Even though at times I took you for granted and caused you pain and anger, I hope you forgive me.

My dear Neda and Nema. My dear little Neda, Nema, whom I have not yet met or seen a picture of, I hope when the time is right Farah and the family will tell you about my life, legacy, and death. Please know that I have not been after power for myself and only intended to serve my people and my country. I hope you remember me that way and learn from my mistakes so that you can become a worthy and good person for your country and faith. I wish you happiness and success.

My dear parents, here is all I have, which is nothing but debt. Please pay them off, and add this to all the troubles I caused you in life:

1. I owe fifty thousand tomans to each of you. I hope you can forgive me.
2. I owe ___ some money for my dental work. I beg you to calculate it and pay him back.
3. I bought a car eight years ago, from my high school and college friend. I've paid the car payments, but I think I might owe him money, too. Please pay him.
4. During my years of friendship with Rostam, he gave me money in order to help the Confederation, but I don't know how much of it was spent for my personal use. It must be calculated and paid back.
5. If there is anyone among the relatives to whom I owe money but cannot remember, please find out and pay them.
6. If you'd like to keep any of my possessions as keepsakes, please do, but after that, my dear Farah is in charge and free to do whatever she wants with my things. I beg you to please

give her all the rights and responsibilities of the children's care and education. Always treat and love her like your own child and remember that she's done so much for me. At the same time, she should be free to continue her life. When she is mentally and emotionally ready to start a new life, I expect you to help and guide her. Please know that I have become a Muslim, and if it were up to me, I would raise my children Muslim until they grow up and personally accept Islam.

    To Mother, Father, Amu, Ameh, __, __, Farah, Neda and Nema, __, __, __, __, __, and __ [13]:

Don't hold any anger and grudge against the Islamic Republic; a government must be strong from inside in order to fight the Western imperialism and the aggressive Soviet Union. In recent years, different Iranian organizations have acted against the republic based on their own beliefs and desires.

Without exception, Marxists acted against the government. We were one such group. Even if a person has not personally fought against the Islamic government, he must take responsibility for the actions of his entire organization. This was the case for me.

After this, may the society and the great people of Iran achieve more unity, victory, and happiness.

[. . .] I believed in and had a special love for the leader of the revolution, Imam Khomeini. Many victories were achieved because of the existence of such a

---

13   I still have family in Iran, family who return to Iran, and family members who've renounced and rejected my father entirely. I don't want to erase them from this letter so I've left blanks to indicate he included them.

character, the revolution, and the Islamic Republic. I hope God protects him for the revolution and for the hardworking people of Iran.

I apologize for the sorrow and pain I caused you and ask you to forgive me and pray to God for my forgiveness. I send you my love.

I ask you not to cry for me. Hold your heads up and know that I don't have the slightest fear of death. At last, sooner or later, we will all die. It's not very complicated, and we shall meet again.

The son, the brother, the husband, the father, and your friend, dear ones,

Faramarz Toloui-Semnani

~

Washington, DC, and Berkeley, California, 1983

The year before my father died, one of his and my mother's friends was killed, and every day and night for a week afterward, people would gather together and talk. They'd share the tiniest, minutest memories. They'd laugh or cry together.

But now, there was nobody for my mother to talk with about her husband. Anything they had done together that seemed funny or clever or brave wouldn't resonate with people like her sister and brother-in-law, who were on the other side.

She wanted to talk about her husband: his character, his sense of humor, his intelligence, his charisma, his attractiveness. My father was good with his hands. He was good with his mind. He made her feel secure. My mother was the kind of person who lived each day for the pleasure of telling her partner all about it in the evening. For twelve years she had felt that as long as he was somewhere breathing, she was safe.

The week after my father was killed, Khaleh, Reza, and my mother went to the movies and saw *Sophie's Choice*. My mother cried through it. She only wanted to hear about people coping with tragedy, people who had lost a loved one. When there was news that 220 American marines had been killed in a Beirut, Lebanon, bombing, my mother felt that their families knew the pain she was feeling.

When she learned about how Princess Grace died, she thought the same thing.

Whenever she heard something tragic, she felt a jolt of relief that she wasn't alone.

After my father died, my mother would wake up in the middle of the night, terrified of a nuclear attack or a war breaking out.

A few days after the executions, the Confederation members in the States wanted to hold a memorial for the twenty-two people who had been killed. My mother agreed to go, but she refused to speak.

She flew from DC to Berkeley for the memorial held at the university's auditorium. The room was filled with people; speeches were made. The organizers had pictures of each executed person enlarged and posted in the auditorium. How surreal it was to be saying goodbye in the place where it had started. How appropriate.

"One other memory I have," my mother said in the 1991 interview, "was about this young kid, who couldn't have been more than twenty, and was secretly in love with Ameh. One day he came to our house [in Tehran] with a pail of cherries. He'd started washing the cherries, and I remember we were eating cherries all day long and joking and laughing. We'd be laughing so much we'd be rolling on the floor.

"This young boy who'd used the excuse of bringing us cherries from his home to see Ameh and . . . they executed him. There were a number of them like this boy. Who didn't participate in Amol, who were no more than sympathizers. I've even forgotten his name now.

"Anyway," my mother said. "That's what happened."

~

Missouri, June 2018

I drove down Route 66 and stopped at a roadside store that promised a wide selection of swords, daggers, and throwing stars. I let myself linger over self-published volumes on how to disappear and fall off the grid without leaving a trace.

I asked the teenage girl with long, dishwater-blond hair sitting behind the counter if anyone bought the blades.

"Sometimes," she said. "They were popular a few years ago."

"Why?" I asked.

She shrugged.

I stopped at the Vacuum Cleaner Museum in Saint James, a surprisingly extensive one-room museum.

This is my collection, the curator told me. He walked to the back of the space, where a round vacuum was up on one wall.

This was the first vacuum I ever fixed, he said, looking fondly at the round, mint-green machine. He was five years old when he saw the thing tossed in a neighbor's trash pile—a GE Roll-Easy from the 1950s, made for rolling faithfully behind the user as they went through the house, up and down stairs. He dragged the vacuum home, and he and his father spent days fixing it until it ran again.

It was a way to spend time with my father, he said. When he was seventeen, he started selling vacuums door to door, still later he opened a business repairing the machines, and over the course of his life, he was gifted vacuums enough to fill several museums. Then, some years ago a small manufacturer asked if they could study his collection. In exchange, they would give him the first floor of their factory to turn into his museum.

The Roll-Easy still works, he said. All the vacuums in the museum did, even the ones from the early 1900s. He used each one in its turn to clean the space.

God, how lucky, I said. *What if you hadn't run across that vacuum?*

I was looking at the man who had once been a small boy, pulling at his destiny hidden in the belly of a broken green machine. How beautiful that, folded into this thing he loved, was his relationship with his father.

I was an asshole for taking the great complicated and winding path he'd traveled and straightening it out as I wrote about fate, destiny, and paternal love. I'd made it pat. I turned him into a character in my story.

He kept on talking, telling me about his brother, and the best vacuum ever made (a Kenmore).

The next morning, I went for a quick hike before leaving for home. I stepped on the trailhead from the parking lot and walked on the wide path through a green glade, which morphed into a canopied forest. Then, the path narrowed and was lost along the jutting rock face. But eventually I began the final ascent to the mountain's summit. The earth up there was made of the Devil's honeycomb, maroon-colored, hexagonal rhyolite rock formations, which, if looked at from above, were reminiscent of the labored output of an army of honeybees.

At the mountain's top, it felt as if the world had quieted and the air stilled. The mountain and these crystalline formations were the creation of a volcanic explosion that had occurred some 1.48 billion years ago. The Ozarks spread around me, and the only sound was the buzz of a flying insect. I waved my hand in front of my face and then turned in a slow circle to take in the view: rich emerald-green against a brilliant azure sky. The view in autumn must be a kaleidoscope of bright yellow and deep red-orange leaves. I wondered if my father and his friends had ever borrowed a car to come here on a bright and crisp day.

Had he considered how much of America had been negotiated from the land below? From where I was standing to the curve of the horizon was the rich rural playground of Huck Finn, Tom Sawyer, and their creator, Sam Clemens. It was the land where the First Nations had lived and then were forced to leave; all around me was the intersection of east, west, north, and south and the farthest edge of the American Civil War.

"It feels like you're here," I said out loud, though I knew I was alone. I sat down and pulled my knees up to my chest. It felt like if I stretched my fingers, I could latch on to the contours of his frame. As a child, as a teenager, and through most of my adulthood, I would talk to my father before I went to bed. I would tiptoe outside or find a place where I could see the night sky, and I would tell my father about my day and my seemingly unending list of worries.

If I belonged to any sort of religion, I would have been a blasphemer, because these one-sided conversations mimicked prayer. When I was twelve and always sad, I'd talk to my father's ghost, which wasn't a spirit but more like an absence of space following me around. When it became overwhelming, I would pull up the red blinds in my room, lie on my narrow twin bed, close my eyes, and stroke my own hair. I'd whisper comforting words softly so neither my mother nor my brother could hear.

I kept talking to him through college and into the early days of my mother's illness. Eventually, it was less talking and more directing all my sadness, rage, and anger toward him for having left us. As my mother got sicker, my life narrowed to doctors' visits, postsurgical care, and living with a dying person. The time for prayers and ghosts had come and gone. I didn't have time for him.

And yet, the moment I arrived in Missouri, I felt him with me. His presence was everywhere and made me slightly giddy, like being with an old friend after a long time away. He was all around me, pulling me along further and further.

On the top of the mountain, I closed my eyes. I let myself imagine a different kind of life. The two of us on this mountain with a country at our feet.

Time stopped. A beat. Then time started.

I brushed the dust off my shorts and clapped my hands together, then I made my way down the mountain.

PART III

PART III

FOURTEEN

Today is thirty-eight years since my father was killed. Thirty-eight years since I saw him, touched him, and was able to push my body against his. Tomorrow, he'll have been dead longer than he was alive. And look. I'm still grieving, though the shape of it has changed with the decades.

Recently, someone asked me if I remembered when I first learned how my father had died, and I told them no. My brother and I always knew he was killed—though the particulars of how were filled in over time. Even so I don't remember anyone dwelling on the mechanics of his murder: shot down by a firing squad. And I don't remember who finally told me that was how it happened.

It feels like the knowledge has always been there, hanging like a backdrop in the background of my mind. For years, I'd think of my father, blindfolded, facing a line of guns. His body jerking before it finally crumpled into a pile on a cold patch of ground. Now, at least, I don't need to think about those details. Now, I can skate over the specifics when I think about his killing.

After a parent dies—or truly, after the death of anyone who grounds you to this world and helps you make sense of it—life separates into a before and an after. When I lost my father, I also lost the family I knew, and the country I understood. For a little bit, I lost the familial and cultural connections that could help me grieve an absence that felt so large as to be unthinkable, as to be absurd.

For a time, after a loss that big, the world and one's place in it are entirely unstable.

For a time, the world and one's understanding of it are completely unreliable.

When you're a child—and later, I learned, when you're an adult—grief will fill you up. It will take up your whole body and ooze from your pores. The profundity of loss can and will change you, because it challenges you to make sense of a new world order. It challenges you to be resilient.

Before my father died he taught me about stories. I'm told we spent most days together and he would draw cartoonlike characters and tell me stories to match them. Pages of drawings and hours of stories. Later, when I came to the United States, my grandmother would gather me on her lap and we would look at the newspaper's funny papers. She would point at a frame of a comic strip, I would tell her stories to match the picture, just as my father had taught me.

Telling stories, not once but over and over and over again, was how I learned to try and make sense of my new reality. Even as a child, I used this skill and drew from my deep connection with my father and our life together to build myself a new life.

As I grew I used stories to find connections between myself and my parents' younger selves. I tried desperately to understand, quite simply, why my father was killed. I wanted to make peace with all of this so badly that I eventually went back to Iran in my early twenties and lived with my family there in the same apartment where my father had been taken away.

This constant interrogation—my constant questioning and pushing to understand—was what my mother called my father's ghost. The questions haunted me, yes, but they were also what kept my father in my life all these years.

I've spent my life learning how to live in the aftermath of his death, of their revolution, and of extraordinary loss. I've spent my life learning how to metabolize grief even as I exalt in being alive.

My parents' presence and their absence shaped me so deeply and so well that I don't know how else to explain it except to show how it happened. So, I've woven pieces of me that were left behind in journals, letters, emails, and articles. I've chosen words from the first time I tried to write this book when I was eight years old until now to reveal a child as she grows up in the shadows of everything that's come before her. I've also included my mother's words to give a sense of who she was and of who we were as mother and daughter.

This way of coping, exploring, and indulging my curiosities has never left me. It's a fundamental part of who I am and how I navigate my world. It's why I am the person I am. It's why I am a writer.

~

Aged Eight

1987–1988 Grade Three
My Dad
written and illustrated by
Neda Toloui-Semnani Garrett Park Elementary School

My Dad died when I was three. I am very sad my
Dad died.
He lived a good life. He was a good man.
He fought for freedom in Iran. He was 38 years
old when he died.

He may not be with me, but I have his memory in
my heart, and I still love him as much as ever.
When I look at his pictures, memories come back
to me.
Standing by the beach brought back memories of
my mom and dad running across the shore
with me.
Although I know those days are gone, I still love
him and will always remember him.

Aged Fourteen

October 28, 1993—Diary

A lot of things have changed this year: I have a great relationship with
my family. For once in my life, I have <u>real</u> friends. Things are changing
every day: some for the best, others?

Well, you know.

I always say, "Things will end up as they should."

March 25, 1994—Diary

I watched a movie tonight and, as I was waiting for it to rewind, I
started looking through the bookshelf where I saw a book called, <u>The
Oxford Guide to Word Games</u>. Wouldn't it be funny, since they have
guides for everything if they had one guide for the heart and soul and
right and wrong? Would the guide be able to bring people together?
Would it be able to stop starvation and war?

I thought about my family. Each member is different as can be. We fight. We fight long and hard and disagree over many things, but we still love and accept each other. No guide could have taught my family to be peaceful. We needed to struggle. I guess, <u>no</u> guide will lead humanity to peace. We need to find our own way there.

I came to the conclusion that there's no completely *right* or completely *wrong*. There are only four things that can bring goodness into the world: acceptance, love, hope, and understanding.

By *acceptance*, I don't mean condoning someone's actions or beliefs, but understanding the cause or the root of their actions or beliefs. We have to <u>accept</u> there are different sides to situations. Once we can accept people as they are, then the other three things (love, hope, and understanding) will follow.

If each person in the world acted like family, a true and loving family, and they wished acceptance, love, hope, and understanding for everyone, then all the bad would stop. People would start paying attention to what is actually important: living and loving.

August 6, 1994—Diary

At the end of my first half day in California. I didn't realize how much I missed my father's side of my family, especially my grandfather, Bubada.

August 6, 1994—Diary

Momana, Dad's mother, is always crying. I want to make her stop. I want to make her see all the stuff she's missing out on in life. But she can't see or listen.

Aged Fifteen

February 13, 1995—Diary

I *am* starved for guidance. I need to believe in somebody or something. First, the person I need to believe in must have my same deep-rooted beliefs. Disagreeing is okay, but always arguing or always disagreeing isn't what I need.

I need someone who will listen to me and take me as I am, flaws and all. Someone who doesn't give advice in response to everything I say. Is that even possible?

God forbid you don't need someone's help and just need their support. Sometimes you feel hurt and confused and want to hide under the bed, curled up like a cat, and lick your wounds.

You can't. The world keeps turning with or without you. The problems of the world are much larger than your day-to-day struggles, even though sometimes it doesn't feel that way.

Sometimes my problems feel too big.

March 26, 1995—Diary

Mom tried to wake me up this morning. I told her to give me ten more minutes. Ten minutes later, Nema comes into the room.

"Neda, wake up!" he said. "Mom's dad is dead."

I thought he was saying, "Mom died. Mom died. Mom's dead."

When I woke up wider, I realized what he was saying, and I was a little relieved.

At the house, my mom and aunt clung to each other and sobbed. They all looked so much older suddenly. Tired with puffy eyes and tear-stained faces. I did not want to be there at all. Watching adults acting human is not my idea of an ideal Sunday morning.

Outside the skies were clear. Warm sun, soft wind. Nema and I backed out of the house and ran as fast as we could down the street until we got to the park. We walked toward the creek, ducking under branches, making our way over the rocks.

I picked yellow flowers, then we went back.

March 31, 1995—Diary

I believe when people die, we should gather, wear all white, and talk and laugh about their life. We should remember the person in all their glory. But I'm a kid. What do I know? Doing that wouldn't be proper or respectful or whatever.

I'm learning that death is an ending and a beginning. It is losing a person and finding them. It's tragically grace filled.

April 19, 1995—Diary

I went on my nightly walk. It was warm, the stars were shining brightly against the dark sky. None of the stories of how the stars came to be feel right to me tonight.

I chose my own: each star is a union of two people who come together and fall in love so deeply and powerfully that their souls come together in a breathtaking explosion. They weave together and spiral upward and take their place in the heavens. Two become one burst of light that never dies. A star of love.

Tonight, I named one star for my mother and father, for Cupid and Psyche, for Romeo and Juliet.

July 7, 1995—Diary

I've never taken the train before. I thought it would be like the train cars of the 1930s and 1940s. Glamorous people, huge seats and sleeper rooms.

Instead, it's bleak. Nothing like I imagined. No one turned glamorous as soon as they climbed on board. This train has a used-up look and a dried-up smell, nothing really offensive, but you just know as soon as you step out of the car, you'll be free of the funk. There's nothing about this to make you want to curl up in your seat and purr happily.

I don't really mind. I'm on my own. I'm alone and content to be. For one week, I'm going to be part of this group who works in New York City and lives in a homeless shelter—a different one every day for a week. Then we'll spend a week reflecting on the problem of homelessness in our country.

I'm anxious to get there and to meet everyone in the group, but at the same time I'm worried: What should I expect? What should I brace myself for? Do I try and absorb the struggles of the homeless people we'll be serving, or should I detach myself like a reporter? How will I know what to do?

July 9, 1995—Diary

I watched the guests streaming into the wide lunchroom and my heart jumped into my throat and stuck there. I couldn't breathe. I kept thinking about how most of these people didn't have homes. What could I do? How could I help? I had an urge to run out the door. To run anywhere. To run everywhere. To get far away.

I didn't want to see their faces. I didn't want to look into their eyes. I didn't want to hear their voices. I didn't want a group of people, who've been relatively unreal to me to become a reality. I can't explain how mixed up I felt.

Then it passed, and I was curious. I wanted to walk up to each person and talk to them. I wanted to walk in their shoes and see through their eyes. A group sang to us to thank us for coming. People smiled at me. They spoke to me and we shared small moments, small considerations.

I helped prepare food in the kitchen and put utensils on trays. In a small way, I contributed to making sure people were getting nourishment and love.

July 11, 1995—Diary

We worked at a soup kitchen that was bad. It was disorganized and really dirty. The dining room was dark and musty; the service was impersonal. It's no wonder the guests were defensive and hostile. There was a fight between two of the volunteers who worked at the site.

I learned a lot from my day here. Mostly how not to treat people and that we can show love and respect by providing a comfortable and warm environment.

July 28, 1995—Diary

"We no longer believe that the way to bring about change is by words or persuasion . . . , it is by example." Michael Rossman from *Berkeley at War: The 1960s*

Aged Seventeen

March 24, 1997—Diary

I'm now a fourth-quarter Senior. I find myself growing increasingly more irritable. I have all this energy, all these feelings filling me. Piling high and over me. Sometimes I feel like I'm about to explode. I keep telling myself: Hold on a few more months, then you're gone. Hold on until then.

There is a world outside my own. One I can just barely see, barely brush my fingers against. Will I be okay? Will I make it? Will I fight for what I believe in? Will I get the things I want? What if I lose everything?

I have fought hard to develop into a woman who is strong, secure, feminine, and masculine. But what if she isn't enough? What if it all hurts too much? What if it is too hard? What if she crumbles? What then?

March 26, 1997—Diary

Have you ever felt like if someone saw you right at that moment, their breath would fly away? Your eyes catch the light just right, your hair swirls. It's fascinating: you move your hair from side to side and look at your face in a reflection. Even your flaws look okay.

You haven't changed or morphed or anything. You are who you've always been except your view has altered, slightly.

There is no flash of lightning or clap of thunder, it's a subtle change. It's just that the wind moved and there's an epiphany.

March 28, 1997—Diary

I drove to New York today and I will probably drive home tomorrow. I feel like I am searching for something. I keep stretching to grab it, my fingers barely graze it.

May 19, 1997—Diary

I went alone to prom and had more fun than anyone. I ran around to my different groups of friends. I tried not to sit still, because if I did, I would remember that this is a last.

Taylor said I looked beautiful. We all did. There was something about the way everyone looked that night. Something about their faces.

I want to remember them this way, before they run headlong into life.

June 12, 1997—Diary

I graduated today. Tomorrow I will try and remember everything I did when I thought I knew everything and when I thought I was independent, but relied on everyone. It's so hard to let go when you want to keep everyone and everything. It's so hard when you can't absorb enough, and the moment vanishes. It's always too late.

I felt my father was with me. I felt him smiling and shaking his head like he couldn't believe how much I had grown and how far I had come.

June 20, 1997—Diary

Before I left for London, I drove to the Delaware beaches by myself. I was brimming over. Excited to get into the water. It wasn't terribly cold, but the waves were rough. It took me a while to dive under. The waves seemed huge and overpowering but once I dove it was really easy to ride swells and swim. It was a beautiful day and I did fine.

But the moment before I went under was really scary. I guess that's how I feel now: apprehensive about leaving everything I'm used to behind.

June 22, 1997—Diary

I believe I'll take to traveling. I saw two rainbows yesterday. I think that's a good omen.

Aged Twenty

Undated—1999

I got an assignment to write a fictional family history on the Vietnam wars, from the 1880s to 1975. And I did. It's hardly Dickens or Hardy or Woolf, but it's a real, proper story.

Aged Twenty-One

August 15, 2001—Diary

I pulled into the parking lot and it smelled like the end of summer. I can't really describe the smell, but it's always there this time of year.

August 18, 2001—Diary

This summer Khaleh gave me a lot of her old clothes. I spent hours putting together these outfits and—how can I explain it?—I felt my mind begin to clear. I began to open up. I let in color and texture and pleasure.

That same day, I decided to devote myself to Mom and Nema. I started to clean my room. I discarded piles and piles of stuff.

August 25, 2001—Diary

Nema left for Ohio this morning. As we finished packing the truck, he and I sat down and smoked a cigarette. We were both surprised by how much we were going to miss each other. He's one of the most fun people to talk to, even if the bulk of our conversation is about *The Simpsons*. Sometimes it's funnier to hear him quote it than to watch the show itself.

It was really hard to watch him leave, so I got out of the house as fast as I could, because without Mom and Nema there it felt so empty and soulless.

Such a contrast to the past couple weeks when it felt like home, even with all the fighting. It wasn't a place I wanted to run from.

August 27, 2001—Diary

I've gotten into this weird habit of flipping coins. Like: Do I call him? Heads for *yes* and tails for *no*. It's like an oracle of sorts.

September 16, 2001—Diary

The knot in my stomach is getting tighter. I remember thinking that something was coming. Something big and exciting, but now it's all profound and unspeakable.

I feel like everything is unclean. Covered with grime and dust and blood. Everything is contaminated now. People keep talking about how Americans have remembered what it means to be American again. They keep saying there's this feeling of unity and patriotism that's pervading the nation, blanketing everything and everyone.

But I can't feel it and questioning my country, a country I love, makes me feel lonely, treasonous, and guilty.

Alice came down to stay with me. Her apartment was four blocks from the towers. It seems like one by one the buildings in lower Manhattan are collapsing and we're hoping hers won't be one of them.

She saw everything: the second plane, bodies falling away from one certain death to another. She heard the building groan and collapse, snapping like matchsticks.

She stood transfixed, watching without understanding what was happening. It's crazy that people—not countries or gods—unleashed so much horror.

In the back of my head, there's a constant prayer running in a loop. I don't know what else to do.

September 24, 2001—Diary

The night before the attacks I had this ominous feeling. I couldn't sleep. I worked myself up and I was terrified. I got down on my knees—*in the parking lot behind my building*—and I prayed.

That night, I slept on the couch so I could see the sky through the sliding doors. This way I can talk to Dad until I fall asleep—like he can see me better this way.

Aged Twenty-Three

Washington, DC, Spring 2003

My Dearest Neda,
You are in my thoughts every day. I want you to know that I love you deeply and completely. You are, after

all, my baby and you embody my most cherished and happiest memories. All the years that you and Nema were growing up and the three of us were our unit, you were my rock—the child who gave me strength. I always had, and still do, enormous faith in your inner strength, and your good judgment and your ability to find your way around and through tough times.

Neda, my love, my daughter, I want you to know that I love you unconditionally. I want more than anything to be a source of support for you, but only as you judge you want and as you guide me. I know you need your space and to explore your inner self—to discover the source of your pain and current sadness in order to set a course for your future. I want you to know that I am willing, at any point, to participate in your journey to determine my role in creating the pain you feel. I again will look to you to let me know when and how or if you want me involved in this part of your journey.

Nema has mentioned he may want to stay in Ohio for summer school, but I hope he comes home before term starts.

I miss my children. I feel their absence now more than I did when you both were in college. But I know both of you must discover your life and must have space and time to do so. I had many years to find my space and I'm glad I had it, without my mother's interference. You should have your time as well. Don't worry how long it takes. It may be a short period, or it may take time—don't rush it.

For my part, I am ready to help in whichever way you need, but I will take my cues from you. Again, please know that you're in my heart and will always be my Nedushka, my Nedush, my baby.

All my love,

Mom

September 26, 2003

Dearest, dearest Neda,

I've been counting the hours since you left, thinking now she is getting on the plane, now she is fastening her seatbelt, now they are over the Atlantic, now she is getting on the plane to Tehran. Remember the song . . . "When I get to Albuquerque she'll be sleeping."

I hope you arrived okay without much trouble, though I suspect I will have talked to you by the time you read this email. I hope you get a chance to communicate with email often, since it's so convenient. Khaleh called me when I got home to say, "your place was empty . . . *Jayeh Neda khalist.*"

I agreed with her. I even went to your room and walked about breathing your scent. I just want you to know that you're in my heart and in my mind—always.

Write to us as often as you can.

All my love and lots of kisses,

Mom

September 27, 2003

Hi Everyone,

I keep stepping out onto the porch and thinking, "Am I really here?"

At the Tehran airport, the guard in the passport control booth asked, "Did you leave the country illegally?"

"Yes," I said, "but I was two."

Ameh jumped back into the booth to say, "She was only two."

The very Islamic looking guy said, "Lady, two or ten, illegal is illegal." He's not wrong. He let me through. I smiled very sweetly and said thank you . . . and walked out of customs straight into the arms of twenty relatives.

Day one has come and gone, I haven't done much yet but hang out with my cousin, who is beautiful, kind, sweet and patient, and my grandmother, who is crazy, hilarious, and lovely. My Persian is rapidly improving. I can feel a difference even after a day.

I have so much I want to tell you guys about how I am feeling. The strangeness of it. How it feels seeing the emotions pouring out of everyone. No one thought we'd make it back.

September 28, 2003

Hey Neda, my lovely,

I have to sit on my hands to keep from stalking you by phone. Khaleh keeps reminding me that I must leave you alone and let you become "independent." I know she's right, but I can't help it. I want to be there to see everything and watch you as you become reacquainted with this important part of your life, your past, and, I hope, your future.

You must be in Kerman by now. That will be a whole new experience—another world and perhaps the more exotic of all. If you last in Kerman with good cheer and find the experience enjoyable, I'll know you'll survive your time in Iran.

Write all about everything, every detail.

My love to you, my lovely,

mom

October 4, 2003

Dear Elana,

Kerman is a desert city surrounded by these imposing mountains that look smaller than they actually are because they're bare. Although the summer is over, it's still hot—though if I could've worn clothes appropriate for the desert it probably wouldn't have been as bad.

The beauty of the desert is in its contrasts. In the middle of the dust and uniform beige, there are oases, wildflowers, morning glories and roses, brilliant against the beige backdrop.

I was in Kerman with my uncle, Daii. We stayed in the family's new house, just across the courtyard from the old, which is now just rubble because of an earthquake that hit a long time ago, when I was a baby, I think. There are ruins all over the town and its outskirts. A shadow of the old aristocracy. Everyone's trying to hold on to land, and by extension they're trying to hold on to some semblance of a life that only exists in stories.

Everyone here seems to know the knots and twists of the family tree going back four generations. While I'm completely unaware, making mistakes and not understanding or getting the intricacies.

Last thing, I went to lunch today in a tea house in the Kerman bazaar. It felt like I was having déjà vu until I realized I was remembering a picture with my parents. I was sitting where whoever took the picture was sitting. *Click.*

October 15, 2003

Dear Everyone,

I spent the first week here traveling through Kerman province, visiting my mother's family, and seeing our lands for the first time.

Our last full day my uncle, Daii, his friend, and I went for a day trip to Jiroft, where our citrus orchards are. With two hours of sleep and a mild hangover, I step out of the car dusty and a little bit grumpy. From the moment we had gotten close to the orchard, the workers had literally been pushing each other to get close to Mr. Daii Khan.

I leaned against the car looking over the orange and grapefruit trees. Scattered throughout the orchard were date trees that look like fat palms with clusters of red Christmas ornaments hanging from the center. The bush in front of me started shaking and a short man leapt out from behind. He had small birdlike eyes and a wrinkled face, though he couldn't have been more than thirty-five. He looked like the black dates I eat each day with my tea.

He was wearing faded, dusty gray pants rolled at the ankles with a blue shirt. His unraveling gray turban sat crooked on his head. He raced by me, jumped into the air, and landed with a thud before rolling through the dirt sideways, stopping at Daii's feet. He grabbed my uncle's hand and kissed it ferociously.

I looked at one of the workers standing near me and laughed. He started laughing, too. I have no graceful aristocratic manners. I snort and joke with peasants. Silly girl.

Afterward, we drove across the desert to Bam city and I saw my first mirage. It was the ocean to the right of the road. I saw the waves lapping the shore and the white sea foam curling up and spraying the sand. I swear—I could almost hear the crash.

My uncle said that because of the weather, I wouldn't see a good one, but I loved the one I saw.

October 15, 2003

Neda jan:

Always the editor that I am, I can't keep myself from making a few comments. If you reread your email you may be able to edit them, so all parts are clear, particularly for people who are strangers to the scenes you're describing.

For example, it would be helpful for us to get a better picture of Jiroft and other places you're seeing— the orchards, the peasants. I don't really know the politically correct term for peasants, but I believe that is still the term. I could be wrong. Finally, remember to use "too," as in "also," rather than "to."

I'm sure I've pissed you off royally by my editorial comments, but I always think great writers need great editors, so here I am to peer over your shoulder.

Write to me about everything. You can't imagine how much I wait for your emails or calls. But since I can read and reread your emails, I would love to get long emails, like the one you sent.

Give my special love to everyone.

All my love,

Mom

October 22, 2003

My dearest Neda,

We had such a lovely talk last night. I felt like you were sitting beside me.

I keep racking my brains for interesting things to write to you, but life here is so mundane—news is still the same awful stuff about the bullying of this administration, though it seems they're now trying to clean up some of their mess.

This year, it is going to be just Nema and me of our little threesome for Thanksgiving. We're going to really miss you. But as you know, having said this, you can't imagine how excited I am for your experience there.

I know you know this already, but experience in living in a place like Iran will mean a lot in your life. It is a very complex place, with a web of social rules, not to mention other issues, and in order to learn the unwritten rules and to get through the maze, you will need to mature, become complex yourself, not necessarily in a bad way, but in a worldly way. In effect, this year is a coming of age for you.

I have to go back to work now, but I'm thinking of you all the time. I'll try to call you again shortly.

All my love,
Mom

Aged Twenty-Four

October 25, 2003

Dear Everyone,

I keep seeing these women covered in great chadors, basically these black sheets that cover their whole body and billow in the breeze. I board the bus—pay in the front and board in the back, where the women's section is—and they're there. I walk down the street and see their faces looking out from beneath a glob of black.

The smell of sweaty chadors seems to permeate the air and sink into the fabric of my clothes. I find it oppressive, but what do I know? I am just a visitor here. I can't judge. I can't act without committing to stay.

I've been waiting to feel angry since I got to Iran, and today my anger came smelling sharply like black chadors under the hot Tehran sun.

That night I went to dinner with my mother's cousins. They were all girls or, I guess, women—in their teens to sixty. As they walked into the apartment and circled around each other, one was prettier than the next. I watched them dance, talk, and laugh. They were like the sirens.

They brought me a cake and jewelry for my birthday, and we took pictures. Each woman looked so much like Mom. They looked a little like me.

This is what I mean when I say Dad is with me here, in this place that vacillates between wonderful and traumatizing. His presence is palpable.

I spend the day righteously angry and then comes the night like an answer to the day. Here women in bright colors dance and sing as loud as they can, defiantly laughing with heads thrown back.

I blew out my candles without making a wish because sometimes life is too much. Sometimes everything is right, and you can't wish for anything more.

October 30, 2003

Hi, Neda jan:
You can congratulate me: I was promoted today. Now I have to work harder, rather than take company time to write to you like I'm doing now.

Thanksgiving is approaching and our little family has become smaller with you over there.

Write to me whenever you can. These days, you're my entertainment, as well as my pride and joy—as is Nema, of course. It's just that usually when one of you is on course, the other is driving me up the wall. This must be the first time ever that I feel quite engaged with both of you at the same time—knock on wood.

all my love,

Mom

November 17, 2003

Hi Guys,

Nearly every day I'm learning something new about my father. He's becoming more and somehow less real to me. The stories about him are hilarious and exciting. He's just like I pictured: this crazy, ballsy, wonderful man who risked his own safety for others. I mean of course, no one would say anything bad about him to my face.

I'm learning how damn hard people tried to get my father out of Iran. The amount of money, lots and lots, that they spent and wasted, lost and lost, is only a small issue. The people who promised to get him out, or at least promised to try, stole the money and left my family standing in the snow beside the prison walls waiting for Dad to come. I mean this literally: my uncle and my sweet grandfather standing in the snow waiting.

I keep asking myself, when would I give up? When would I get back in the car and go home? When would I say, I can't do this anymore?

I keep thinking about Dad seeing a picture of Nema who was safely born someplace else. Every time I think of those people who raised Daddy's hopes of getting free, I get so angry I don't know what to do.

But I don't think Dad would have left that place, even if he could, not without the others who were in prison with him.

The one thing I don't do is ask "Why us?" As far as I can tell the answer to that might be, "Because you were strong enough to take it." The other might just be, "Because . . ." It's just stupid.

I'm having dreams of Dad. I don't see his face, but I feel his presence. The other night I dreamt I was walking down the sidewalk in Tehran, then I started spinning. I kept going faster and faster until something scooped me up and cradled me. I just knew it was Dad, felt it in the pit of my stomach. With this invisible Dad, I can go anywhere, I can fly. I am whipping about gaining confidence, doing crazy-ass loops, and flips, sudden changes of direction when suddenly a swarm of wasps came for me. I mean straight for my face. I was terrified, but then I realized my Dad was still with me.

It's irrational but I knew that nothing could hurt me while he was there. I could get stung by the whole hive, but I'd never fall down to Earth. Then I woke up.

December 8, 2003

Hey Everybody,

A few weeks before Thanksgiving I decided that I needed a break from emotional bombardment. As much as I enjoy learning a million new things every day, it's a bit draining, too. I needed to see someone I've known long and well. I needed a tall barstool where I could swing my feet and sip a stout. I emailed

Taylor; the only person I was fairly certain would come to meet me in Turkey with two weeks' notice.

I bought my plane ticket on Iran Air, the airline of the Islamic Republic and the absolute cheapest flight I could find. I picked it because a pot-bellied man told me rather nonchalantly during a recent flight to Shiraz, "These planes crash a lot."

"He's right," said another man who was lifting up the seat where a life vest was supposed to be. "They fall out of the sky."

I figured since Istanbul's been attacked over and over the past few weeks, this plane would be the last place terrorists would target since it's already a death trap and it's only a matter of time before bits and pieces of it fell onto the Alborz Mountains.

I made it to Istanbul safe and sound and spent a week with one of my best friends falling in love with Istanbul's winding cobbled streets. For the first time, I could see how beautifully Eastern and Western cultures could come together.

December 20, 2003

Elana,

I've always felt completely American and, simultaneously, not somehow. Here in Iran, I'm constantly reminded of my otherness, because I was raised in the States, because I'm a woman, because of my family. In the US, I felt an underlying foreignness, but here it's on the surface.

I've been at this conference for the past five days, surrounded by two hundred Iranians from all over the country, from all backgrounds, and it feels like they've all asked me if I'm *doh-raggeh*. Am I mixed? Do I have two-bloods? They insist I come from someplace else.

One guy called me a foreigner. Another woman looked relieved when I told her I grew up in the US as if that explained something.

Anyway, the language barrier is a blessing. It forces me to listen and when I do speak, I have to be simple and concise, which probably explains my long rambling emails.

December 27, 2003

Elana,

We're all okay here. I haven't gotten through to the family in Kerman. Five thousand people are dead, and 30,000 people are wounded[14] after the earthquake hit Bam.

Do you remember I wrote to you about the Arg-e Bam, the fortified city? Two thousand years old and perfectly preserved. Now it's destroyed. Think of all the history we've lost.

There's a blood shortage in the area, the two hospitals are badly damaged. The hardest-hit parts of the

---

14 Seventeen years after the earthquake, in December 2020, the government finally announced the official casualty count: thirty-four thousand people were killed and more than two hundred thousand injured from the quake.

city are, of course, the poorest. People from all over the country have piled into their cars and started driving down to help.

December 27, 2003

Hi Guys,

I thought you might like to know how Christmas is celebrated in the Islamic Republic. Actually, it isn't, except by the Armenian Christians and foreigners, but somehow it felt more like Christmas than I expected. There were trees decorated in store windows throughout Tehran and even in conservative, ancient Yazd, there were a couple of trees in the windows.

Three friends and I decided to throw a Christmas Party at one of their flats. It snowed that night. The red glow of brake lights in Tehran traffic and the rhythmic car horns felt festive.

They had decorated their place with poinsettias, Christmas trees, festive candles, and stockings. There was a lavish dinner. Music turned up. Nonstop dancing. Everyone dripping with sweat.

The first hour, Americans commandeered the stereo and let loose a steady stream of hip-hop, old-school and new. Then, the Turks took control. The Palestinians next, and then the Persians. We were all toppled by the hiccuping English. Everyone kept saying what a good party it was and the four of us kept congratulating ourselves for throwing it.

December 27, 2003

Nedoushi:

I just wrote you a long email, but then when I clicked on send, it disappeared. Needless to say, I'm peeved. My email was very sweet, but now I have to go, so I'll have to package everything as a summary.

I really loved your email. We all love them. They are so entertaining and well written; one can imagine the events you write about. My only suggestion is to do a spell check to make sure some of the really bad misspellings are corrected. Also, remember my pet peeve: "myself and my friends" is a no-no for an English major[15]. "My friends and I" is acceptable.

Call me if you can.

All my love,

your mom.

December 31, 2003

Hi guys,

The devastation from the earthquake has been one of the worst things I've ever seen. It's affected all of us over here. But, like all adversity, a great deal of good comes through, as well.

Yesterday, they found an eleven-year-old boy buried up to his neck in the rubble. Like a character out

---

15   For the record, I majored in political science with a concentration in English literature.

of a Greek myth, he spent the last four days able to breathe but unable to move. When rescuers found him, they asked him how he survived. He said that a little girl, maybe five years old, came to him three times a day. She poured water in his mouth and fed him bits of bread as if he was a wounded bird.

She promised he'd be saved and told him to be patient. The little girl, like the boy, had lost her whole family, but still, she saved him. Can you imagine the spirit, the goodness, the resilience of the girl? She saved him by bringing food and water, yes, but also human connection.

January 21, 2004

Neda jan:
The woman I'm reading about here is not the same one who went to Iran. I will write more later. We are all counting the days till you come home.

All my love,
Mom

January 22, 2004

Momma-jan,
I can feel the shift beginning, the change that starts before you move from one place to another. All my stuff is still hanging in closets and folded in drawers. My desk is stacked with books and snapshots are still on the walls. Books are half read by my bed and my

shoes are still in the shoe shelves. But the person who belongs to all of those things is getting ready to leave.

I went to see Momana last night. Now that the scariness is over, I can tell you about the night before she got sick when everyone gathered around each other for the first time in twenty-two years. Nobody thought we'd be together again, especially not in Iran.

I couldn't get enough of Momana. She was already starting to feel poorly, and I followed her around like a puppy for the evening.

It is funny, I've never felt terribly close to her. I loved her but I didn't understand her. She annoyed me and scared me a little bit. But since coming here, I've learned so much about her. I love her sense of humor, the way she's able to laugh at herself.

It was just the two of us in the hospital room one day and she said, "I don't want to go away."

She started crying. She said she had a dream that her father and Bubada were praying on the foot of her bed. I said that they weren't there to *take* her, they were there to *help* her. She grabbed my hand and said, "I am not a scared person, Neda. I have never thought of myself like that."

"I know," I said. I told her to concentrate on the fact that Bubada had come such a long way to help and she must meet him halfway and get better.

We went to see Daddy's grave a few days later, as soon as we got to the gravesite, they called to tell us she'd been released. And then last night we're sitting around the table and her blue eyes are bright and focused. She was making us laugh.

It's a sign, I think, that maybe it's okay for me to leave.

February 1, 2004

Hi Momma,

We're off work today because the Imam Khomeini came back to Iran 25 years ago. I don't know what else to say about that, but you should see it here. There are posters everywhere. Khomeini's all over the TV. They keep replaying the footage of when he landed. In ten days, it'll be the anniversary of the revolution. Think about how much has happened between then and now. It's crazy to me that I am a child of this revolution. My life began when this regime was born.

What have I learned since I landed here? That it's easier to see the bad than acknowledge the good. It's easier to judge than to empathize.

I love you, my beautiful Momma . . . I have so much that I'm saving up to tell you in person.

xoxoxoxoxo

Neda

February 2, 2004

My dearest Neda,

I love talking to you, and even better, receiving these letters. I can't tell you what they mean to me. They're full of discovery—they radiate with youth, energy, and hope.

I remember myself, when I finally got out of Monterey, where I had been depressed for so long, and so lonely, and started my college life. I felt a cloud lifting from over my head and sensed the joy of being young but not a child. Of the world ahead of me, to be discovered and lived. I don't think I ever returned to my old depressed self again, though I certainly had my blue days, even my blue periods.

I think the same is happening to you. You've left one place for another, where you've had the space and opportunity to challenge yourself and be yourself and you like what you see, and others seem to respond.

Lots of love,

mom

Found, not dated
Farah Ebrahimi's Story

In early 2004 I began to feel pain on the left side of my pelvis, close to my lower bowel and rectum. The pain persisted until I had to take Advil in the mornings and evenings to relieve the symptoms. My bowel movements also changed, being more frequent.

In late February 2004, I went to my internist. I always found him to be a good listener. The previous year I had gone to him with some vague symptoms, such as bloating, vertigo, persistent dry cough.

Each time he'd ordered tests: MRI for my vertigo, endoscopy for my bloating, chest X-ray for my cough. Each time, the results were normal.

I think this may have made him less concerned when I went to him with another vague symptom: pelvic pain radiating through my lower back. He assured me it was nothing serious—probably internal hemorrhoids, since I had a history of hemorrhoids from my first pregnancy, though they were never internal.

He advised me to continue to take Advil, which I did.

March 15, 2004—Diary

I'm anxious to see how Iran will look from here [Washington, DC]. Whether I'll be able to write out of the experiences I gathered. I was loath to mark up this page, but now I've spilled coffee and stained it.

I don't have an idea how to do this. There are a million stories rushing around in my mind: millions of smells and colors are blurred together.

March 30, 2004—Diary

I saw the movie *Eternal Sunshine of the Spotless Mind* today. It's about a man who erases his girlfriend from his memory after he finds out she erased him first. In order for him to get rid of all the bad memories, he has to remember all the good ones.

Eventually, he and she meet again and fall in love—I expect they'll make all the same mistakes now that their old memories are gone. Zapped like flies.

I don't know why they'd do that. We already lose so much over time. I forgot my father. I forgot his look, his smell. What I remember is all nonverbal, nonauditory, nonvisual.

But I'm sure I remember him. If he walked in behind me now, I'm sure I'd eventually remember. It'll be like how I forgot Iran. I forgot the people, but I went back, and I hadn't zapped it all. It was just the slow softening of memory. Images fading and fading until they're just indents on a page.

That's the reason, I think, I hold on tightly to everything because I've forgotten so much of my life. I forgot Dad. I forgot our life.

Maybe I forgot him because there was more I could've done to keep him safe, to convince him to leave? Maybe I could've tried harder to remember him? Maybe my constant and obsessive tributes to him are because I've never forgiven myself.

I've trapped him, in a way. I'm his daughter, not his jailer. I forget that now and again.

Found, not dated
Farah Ebrahimi's Story [continued]

All through March, April, and May, my symptoms got worse. In late June, my GYN did her usual pelvic exam and assured me everything was normal. I asked her to do a test to measure an ovarian cancer antigen. She refused, said it was unreliable. I insisted, telling her I have real pain that is getting worse.

She examined me again, this time more carefully. She hit a spot where the pain was strong and she felt a hardening, but couldn't tell where it was. She ordered a sonogram and agreed to take blood for the test.

The sonogram showed a seven-centimeter mass on my left ovary. The doctor advised that I seek a GYN oncology surgeon immediately and suggested a few names.

After a short search, my husband and I chose a surgeon who performed my surgery on July 14, 2004.

August 2, 2004—Diary

I've had this feeling all year that I'm going to die—or, in any event, that I wasn't going to make it back from Iran. I woke up one night feeling sad and overwhelmed. I called Mom. I told her I was afraid that I was going to die, and I wouldn't get to say goodbye to her.

I can't die, yet. I have the whole world to gobble up and savor. I still have to fall in love. I still have to write my book. I still have to avenge—or make peace. I haven't seen my friends married or Nema. I haven't met their kids.

I want more stories—my own stories. Stories to fill pages in my book. I want a good, kind man to talk with and share life with. I want to learn to surf. I want to run a marathon. I want to act on the stage and see wild horses.

These days I'm just concentrating on being with Mom even though I know she isn't dying—no more than anyone else.

August 2004—Diary

Mom started chemo today and I feel anxious and lost right now like I'm spinning out of control. I have to be careful. I can't afford to get depressed right now. It just can't be a thing right now.

I keep thinking about death in a way I never have before. I keep thinking I'm going to lose everyone close to me.

I'm scared of dying—I know I shouldn't be but I am. I'm scared of the feeling of nothingness, a void—a black hole. I don't want to be alone in this world. My heart is beating so fast. All day long it's been like this.

August 8, 2004—Diary

My safe place, the place I go back to in my mind, is the condo where my mother used to read to us from the *Classic Myths to Read Aloud*. I loved that book. It felt like worlds literally opening and swallowing me up. I remember those nights and then the hot July days when Nema and I chased fireflies and built clubhouses we furnished from old furniture pulled out of dumpsters.

Found, not dated
Farah Ebrahimi's Story [continued]

The surgery was followed by six rounds of chemo—the usual treatments for first-round ovarian cancer. Nothing had spread to the lymph nodes, but there were cancer cells in the pelvic fluid. I was told I had a 67 percent chance of a cure.

The surgery and chemo went well. I tolerated both and went back to work, thinking my nightmare was over. Eleven months later I noticed a small growth on the posterior left side of my vagina. The surgeon saw me immediately and did a biopsy in his office. A week later the results came back—the return of ovarian cancer.

My surgeon had never seen a recurrence on the lower vagina and though the growth was very small, the location made surgery difficult.

Aged Twenty-Seven

September 11, 2007

Mom,
I'm really sorry I haven't had time to email. I have been keeping a journal and constructing emails in my head every minute of the day. Things are wonderful. I love traveling like this [by train through South India].

September 14, 2007—Diary

On my way to the supermarket in Pondicherry, a town on India's east coast, I saw this woman begging on the side of the street. At first, I thought I was seeing a pattern on her blue sari, but as I got closer, I realized what it was really: chunks of her breast that had fallen off her body, or maybe they'd been ripped out. There were flies in her wounds. I gave her some rupees, the rest of my water, and went to find help.

Rue de Bussy, where she was sitting, is filled with doctors, shrinks, and dentist offices, but no one would help me. I didn't know what to do, then I saw a young nun, from Connecticut of all places, waiting for the bus. I cried as I asked her—Sister R—for help.

Together we found a rickshaw driver who spoke passable English and we went to find the woman again. When we found her, he translated. She said she has cancer, but it's gone untreated for so long that her breasts fell off. She went to the hospital for treatment, but they couldn't help her because she needed blood. We think she was trying to beg for money to get a transfusion, but I don't really know. The rickshaw driver took us to the hospital. He didn't charge us anything.

R asks the woman's name and it's Mariam. That's right. She was wearing blue and her name was Mary and today was the Feast of Jesus on the Cross.

Mariam was weak on her feet. She couldn't quite make it up the ramp. She kept getting dizzy as we waited to be admitted. Sister R prayed and I tried not to cry. I sat facing the wall trying to collect myself. There was a sign hanging. It read, "Someday Change will be accepted as life itself."

After a bit, I went across the street and bought cookies, nuts, and these chip type things, and I sat with Mariam as she tried to eat. She was clearly in pain. She was filthy and tired. I opened a water bottle for her. Her eyes got a little watery. I made a face and she smiled. I took a picture of her, sitting on the floor smiling. She was dying, but I wanted a record that she was alive.

After a long time, R brought the Missionaries of Charity, Mother Teresa's order, to help us. They took Mariam for the night, hopefully, longer.

As I walked R to the bus stop, she told me the story of Mother Teresa. How she found a woman covered with maggots and carried her as she looked for help. No one helped until somebody did. She says I've done the same thing.

But one difference between a good person and a saint is that the saint holds a person. They aren't afraid to touch them. I was. I'm so ashamed to admit it, but I didn't want to touch Mariam if I could help it.

I called Mom and woke her up. I was crying so hard I completely freaked her out.

September 17, 2007—Diary

I've completely given in to my instinct to keep moving. I'm not spending more than two days in any one place. If I keep moving, then maybe I'll find what I'm looking for.

I am spending days and days rolling through south India on third-class rail. I'm able to think about the past, to mull over it for as long as I want to. I don't have to talk about it. I don't have to consider anyone else's feelings.

There's relief in being able to get angry and frustrated and not having to explain why.

September 21, 2007—Diary

When I was on the plane from DC to Mumbai, I closed my eyes and I swear I remembered how I felt during the escape, in the dark, on that horse. I remembered wanting someone—Mom, Ameh, Amu—to be with me. I was so scared.

I can remember that feeling clearly. I wonder whether all this time, all these years of missing Dad to distraction wasn't because I felt that if he had been there, I wouldn't have felt alone. I wouldn't have been alone with the smuggler with the dark face. If only Dad had been with me, I wouldn't have been alone or scared.

September 23, 2007

Neda jooni,
Tonight, the family gathered for Nema's birthday. You were really missed. I'm off to bed. Just wanted you to know that we were thinking of you tonight.
Lots of love,
Mom

September 29, 2007—Diary

There is a dull ache, something like a Sunday sadness, that started after I came in from the beach this morning. Josh, my quiet friend and weeklong companion, left today. I feel sad and anxious this adventure is drawing to a close.

Five days until I go home to plan Mom's party and to a feeling of unease and dread. I don't want to go home: not to my family, not to my friends, not to my books or anything else. I don't want to leave. I do not—passionately do *not*—want time to tick on.

I want to stay on the beach with my book. I don't want to plan. I don't want much of anything. I want to stay in the lush, monsoon-soaked hills and look up into a blue-white sky. I want to stay here where I don't have to face Mom dying.

Aged Twenty-Eight

April 21, 2008—Diary

It's strange that what I should take from traveling through India, a country where I was always moving, where I was kept up by families fighting and murders of crows settling in trees, is stillness.

The subcontinent rests. You can still find places to give yourself over to stillness. That was all I was searching for—a place to be quiet.

I was broken when I arrived in Mumbai. Walking out of the airport at midnight, I felt nervous, but I remembered all those times I landed at Tehran's Mehrabad Airport late at night and how I made it home safe.

June 1, 2008—Diary

I can't find my journal, which is appropriate. If you collected all my journals, you'd find I've always been a little bit missing. Now I seem to have misplaced myself completely.

Is this a premonition, a horrible knowing? If she's gone, where will I belong? Whom will I belong to? Will I exist without her?

Something is tapping at me: what are you doing, Neda? Without Mom, what use will you be?

I've always looked down on people who could see they were unhappy but didn't do a thing to change it, but fear and exhaustion have made a coward out of me.

June 7, 2008—Diary

The stories my mother told us when we were small were not made up. Unlike those my grandfather Bubada told us. And unlike him, she didn't gather me close and whisper about magical gardens, talking lions, and hundreds of cousins. Unlike my grandfather, she did not smell like dried leaves.

The stories my mother told me were true and real. They were her own stories of love and loss, but they sounded fantastical in other ways. Her pet, for example, was a fawn her father gave her. It was later killed when a luncheon party grew drunk and bored. Then much later, she got a monkey who fell in love with her mother.

Mom's stories were full of revolution, sadness, and parties. They were so different from our life in small apartments. They may as well have been fairy tales or those myths she'd read aloud, but they were all real and true, though they changed as we grew older. Or, maybe, as we grew older, we just heard them differently.

June 2008—Diary

In a town in Iran, there was a carpet, long and wide, spread across a large room and covered with silver platters of food: fluffed rice drizzled with saffron and butter with the crispy rice from the bottom of the pot. Chicken, lamb, and beef stews were poured into bowls next to plates of fresh herbs, greens, and red radishes. A daily banquet to feed the two dozen people who may or may not appear for the midday meal.

My grandmother sat demurely, presiding over the feast. My grandfather was someplace close by. In some ways, they were destined to fail. They were mismatched. I think they only really loved each other after their divorce. After time and oceans separated them.

But still, in the beginning, life spread out before them like an endless summer fete. Their children were born and attended to with affectionate absentmindedness. First came a daughter, strong and fierce. Then, a long-limbed and mischievous son and, finally, the baby, my quiet and watchful mother.

Aged Twenty-Nine

April 21, 2009

Hi Everyone,

As all of you know, last Wednesday Mom went back into the hospital because of what's turned out to be a bowel obstruction. It's at the bottom of the small intestine blocking the stomach, intestines, and colon from ridding the body of waste materials.

As of now, the surgery is scheduled for 11 am tomorrow. It should be pretty straightforward; the small intestine will be adjusted to bypass the large and will drain out of an artificial opening into a pouch. She'll stay in the hospital for another five days following the operation and then begin to return to chemo and her active lifestyle after a few weeks of at-home recuperation.

Surgery is never the first choice, but she's come through tougher ones over the past five years, so we are confident that she will get through this with the same level of strength, humor, and grace that's been her approach to this entire ordeal.

Mom's been so brave, gracious and playful even. She's a prizefighter and has been exercising steadily, even after five days receiving IV nutrition and has a tube snaking from her belly up to her throat and out her nose. All of us are trying to help her with a zealousness that definitely means we're in her way and in the way of her doctors.

Aged Thirty
Based on events from a week in April 2010.[16]

I was strong-arming my mother, bullying her to put on a dress and take a drive with her brother and sister.

"You're beautiful," I said.

"I am?"

"You are."

"Oh, Nedu. I'm not," she said.

My mother was dying. She was a collection of bony elbows, jutting clavicles, and sunken cheekbones.

Still, she was as beautiful as she was tired and—God, my poor Mom—that day she was exhausted. She would have been more comfortable sleeping with a fresh Dilaudid patch, but I was determined to cheer up a woman who, whether we knew it or not, had only a week left to live.

---

16 Excerpt from the essay "Learning to Live Without My Mother," published in TheWeek.com.

That day, I wheeled Mom into the bathroom. I brushed her hair. Changed her bandages. Doled out pills. I rubbed lotion over her chest and back, down her arms. I carefully applied a bit of lipstick and pinned her curls from her face.

For some reason, I thought that maybe after the makeup, my lectures, some jokes, Mom would feel better. Her one cloudy eye might clear, and she'd hang on for a bit longer.

I thought that if she was happy, and the springtime was beautiful enough, she might not leave us. She might not be so tired, and my family might have just a little more time together.

It was a perfect spring afternoon when my aunt and uncle helped Mom into the car. The three of them set off for what I remember as the last time they had together, just the three of them. It took a superhuman kind of control not to run after them, throw my arms around her neck, and beg her not to leave me behind for the afternoon—to beg her not to leave me ever.

Or maybe, I thought, she will come back happy, refreshed. Maybe all she needed was to get out of the house, to take a drive, to put on lipstick.

But it turns out that when a person is dying, it isn't a thing that springtime or family or lipstick can cheer into reverse.

The day after her drive, or maybe the day after the day after, I walked upstairs and saw Mom sleeping on the adjustable hospital bed set up in the living room. I looked over at my uncle reading on the couch and, suddenly it hit me just how incredibly, stupidly, laughably young and unprepared I was for life without her.

I crawled into the bed hospice had set up and started crying. The crying turned to weeping and the weeping into sobs. The world, and my grief, were too much. I was just a small little nothing of a human.

Then the sobs gave way to howls.

Mom's eyes, half-blind after years and years of cancer, flew open.

"Nedu," she said, her voice a whisper. "Who died?"

"No one, yet," I said.

We looked at each other and I laughed. And she laughed. We held hands and kissed each other, and she told me I was going to be okay.

"Mu, how much do you love me?" I asked.

"Nedu," she said. "I love you as big as the universe, as wide as the ocean and back, forever and always."

"Mu," I said. "I love you as big as the universe, as wide as the ocean, and back, forever and always."

That's when I knew, in that precise moment, that chapter of my life—one where I could always go home, where I got to be a daughter— was over.

It was the last moment I was mothered.

~

Rensselaerville, New York, November, 2018

After my mother's death I lost myself in work. Every morning started with a set of unknowns and it was up to me to pull a story seemingly out of air, to fill the paper's news hole and bottomless, cavernous web. There were moments when I worried if I asked the right questions or if the questions I asked were really answered, and if they had been answered, were they answered well or at least well enough. None of it could bother me for long.

The sun went down.

The deadline dropped, and the day's unknowing had to be smoothed into something like certainty.

Here, the firm active sentence that leads; here, the story folded into a nutshell; and finally the last words, spare and tight, served with a kick.

There's a rhythm to a news writer's day, and although it becomes less predictable the further from the daily cycle one wanders, the rhythm remains: find the story, ask the questions, write down the answers. Use all the different words you know to tell the story. Pull them from the air and extract them from the deep recesses of your mind and then construct them into something concise and clear. This is an antidote to the chaos of real life. The news writer, like a poet, uses structure to put the world in order. A lot can go wrong in the process and the pace is relentless, but there is always a deadline and the quest is the same: find the story, tell it well.

But then I left the paper and one day, I found I couldn't write anything anymore.

This is how you lose your words: At first, they go slow and then they leave faster. You don't notice in the beginning. It's not strange the first time you can't find the words in answer to your own question, but then you can't answer your next question or the one after that.

What is the word for that particular shade of red?

How to describe the flavor of that apple or the way the young man walked?

How can you begin to explain the deep and lingering nature of grief, the kind that tails you for decades?

What are the words to explain the whole of that?

It becomes a great struggle to think of a word, any word at all. Something that could begin a phrase that starts a sentence that could miraculously explode into a paragraph to begin a story.

This is what happened when I left the newsroom to write this thing.

Because there is no rhythm to excavating grief, love, and loss. There is no peg for these things. They exist all around you, me, and us. They seep out and lead to dead lines of inquiry; they bang up against trauma and a primal sadness you don't understand. In order to know these things, I had to travel inside myself and ask: *How do you feel? Why do you feel? When did this all begin?*

Often there were no words to explain; often there weren't enough words to explain; often words weren't enough to explain the quagmire of shit I'd waded into. It was suddenly feelings, all the feelings all around, thrown together into a jumbled morass. It was a great mess with no way out but through.

This is how I lost my words. They began to leave me at the start of my halting journey into the mess of revolution, tragedy, rebuilding, challenge, and adventure. They faded as I reached its hard, pain-filled center.

How do you feel?
Why do you feel?
When did this all begin?

I have learned there are stories that shape us, others that change us, and still others that change with us. The stories I've told here have had many iterations. Over the course of years of reporting and composing, I have jettisoned earlier versions that I had previously accepted as true. I pushed myself to exhume the past. I had to dismantle my child's view of her parents, their revolution, their love story, their heartbreak, and the aftermath we all had to contend with. I picked apart these people, who were no less than my heroes, and I began to rebuild them in context. They emerged as flawed, beautiful, tragic, and fallible. I have dissolved under the weight of their story and the responsibility around its telling. I have broken myself apart into pieces and pulled myself back together.

A friend, a crime reporter and so no stranger to darkness, introduced me to embroidery months into my writer's block. I come from a line of craftswomen. My maternal great-grandmother was a seamstress. Her daughter, my grandmother, embroidered and her work is displayed on her children's walls. These two weren't unique: women across the world, from every culture, have sat down with their needle and thread and stitched their stories. This is how they kept their histories.

I started to embroider. For hours I sat, pushing and pulling the needle until I felt the generations who came before me join me. They flooded the spaces around me. These ancestors, both known and unknown, sat with me as I sutured myself together. My hands cramped and ached. I cried but still I stitched and stitched and stitched myself out of time, out of place, until I felt myself again.

~

Aged Thirty-Nine

April 4, 2019

Whoever you are.
Whoever you are.
Whoever you may be.
Maybe you.
You.

It doesn't matter who you are. I want you, whoever you are, to hear this. Whoever you are, I want you because I need, too. To tell you. I need to tell you a story. To write you a story. I will find you and read you this story. If you can't hear and don't read, I want to show this story to *you*. This story.

But I do want you. I want you to try to read, to see, to listen. To this story about me. It is about me. A little bit. It is a little bit about me. But it isn't only. It is a story about a lot. About a lot of people. People I know and people I never will. It is a story, many stories really, about place and places and some of the people who moved between those. Who moved across those lines. Who crossed those lines.

It is a story. A story about people who moved between places and through time. It is about the past. About journeys I stitched together, scrap by scrap, until the present came through. I wove them into a story; a story I made from wisps gathered from here and there. Wisps threaded through an eye, pierced into a scene, leading from then into later. It might explain how now is. It might explain today some.

That is how this story was built, but it is a tale about. About how things began. I want to tell you what was built and how it was broken. I want to tell you about what we lost. About what I lost. About those lost. I want to tell you all the things lost to me. And to you. About all the loss. Loss that built up like scum on a window and dust on a ledge. I want to tell you about all the loss swept together, piled loss on top of loss until it became: something. Something scattered; scattered like seeds; something like life; something like lives; something like diaspora. I will tell you about those who dispersed. About the dispersed. About those who came apart together and those who then came together. About the ones who lived. Who lived through losing. Who lived throughout the loosening. Who wound themselves tight, who tightened and bruised, who became a new thing. I will tell you some things about them.

I want to tell you all that. And to tell a story about how they made me. How I didn't understand. How I searched through. Through found-lost things. Until I understood. Until I understood something about loss, about things, about the lost things left behind. Then, and I don't know how to do this, but then I want to show you how it went then. How we lived through. How we did that. I want to show you that loss was only some of the story, only part of the story, just a seed of the story, but not the whole of it. Not the whole of our story.

Our story. I want to tell you this story. It is not my story. It is. It is my story, but not only. It is ours. And maybe, maybe, and maybe it is yours, too.

EPILOGUE

Brooklyn, New York, January 20, 2021

Two weeks ago, hundreds of people—mostly white and mostly men—breached the walls of the nation's Capitol building. They broke windows, defecated on the floor, waved their white supremacist flags, beat police officers, and desecrated the halls of the republic. This building wasn't just a symbol of democracy to me, it was the backdrop of so much of my life: I spent my childhood going to marches and inaugurations on its lawns, my high school years monument-hopping in its shadow, and my twenties and early thirties getting lost in the building's crypt-like hallways, first as an intern and later as a reporter. Now, I was hundreds of miles away, watching both my hometown and this building I love under attack as I churned out copy to write and rewrite a nightly news show.

It was an American insurrection, incited by a demagogue and his sycophants, the natural conclusion of the past years. There was nothing particularly exceptional about it except that it happened here and not someplace else.

And here I am pregnant with you, my own son. My Rumi.

This far into my mother's pregnancy with her son, she was scaling mountains. Here I am quarantined from a pandemic, covering the news from a laptop screen, holed up for hours in what will be your room.

Two days ago, we logged on to our computer for your baby shower, and for nearly an hour laughed with far-flung family and friends, who took the time to welcome you from Australia, Great Britain, Iran, and all across the United States. The next day, your father built your crib, put up shelves, and started organizing the boxes of bottles and various baby receptacles into piles around the apartment.

He says he's getting ready for the hundred-year storm.

He says he can't wait to sit around and get to know you.

He says this while taking care of both of us. And watching all of this, I have fallen deeper and deeper in love with him and with you.

Before the 2020 election, I asked him over and over again: Where will we go if the demagogue wins? I pushed and pushed for a plan. I'm a journalist. I'm Iranian American.

"I'm not escaping, pregnant, over mountains," I told your father one night as we filled the dishwasher. "I'm not my mother. If you take too long to decide, I'll leave you."

Even now, an hour before the demagogue leaves the White House and half a day away from the new president's swearing in, I'm not sure what's coming. What I know is that this isn't the end of the bigotry, hate, anger, and wanton disregard for truth and sense. What I know is we're in the middle of a far-right movement that's going to continue to shape-shift over the next few years.

What I know is that you, like your parents and your grandparents and our ancestors before them, will be forced to confront darkness, over and over again.

And you might ask me one day: If you knew it was a pandemic and if you suspected a dark and violent future, then *why,* why did you guys decide to have a family?

It's a fair and good question to ask. One that I understand: I, too, was born in the immediate aftermath of a crisis. In my case, it was a revolution; in yours, it's a confluence of horrors: the legacy of a demagogue, the rise of the far right and conspiracy theories, national economic collapse, and an unchecked pandemic.

But I am sitting in your room, writing to you as you squirm and turn inside me. I chose now to write to you because it's in the moments before I know how today will go, when it's quiet, and I feel something like hope.

Throughout this volume I've asked, *Why?*

Over and over again, like a child I've asked, *Why?*

Specifically, why did my father, your grandfather, decide to start a family knowing what he knew?

And after four decades of questioning, I think it's this simple: Because we all make decisions with the information we have. Because we're imperfect and he was imperfect, and because he loved my mother, he loved me, and he loved my brother. He loved us.

When I was younger, I wanted it to be more complicated. Now, I know it isn't.

I know because I don't know what's coming for us—are we careening into sectarian conflict, a civil war? Or will everything settle down? People scrawled "Murder the Media" on the doors of the Capitol, and yet most journalists keep on working. I would not give up this work, not even for you. Indeed, in order to be the mother I believe you should have, I will not give up this work. This work that is a calling.

I want to watch you grow and to help you grow into the person you will be. I will give up everything for you except that which makes me fundamentally myself: my morality, my exuberance, my resilience, my curiosity, my wonder, and my joy.

These make up the whole of me; I will guard this—the core of me—even from you. Because *this* is the person you will need to show you how to survive what may be a difficult life.

This is what my parents taught me, in their different ways. This is what I will teach you.

On this January morning, at the start of a new administration, it has started to snow. As fat flakes cover the roof and street below, I think it's important I say one thing, just in case it isn't clear: I love my father and I am proud of him. I'm proud of his legacy and am grateful for his ghost, the one who helped raise me. I'm proud to be his daughter and proud that you're his grandson.

This is a choice we all make; indeed it's our first great choice: We choose who we love and how we love. And it's a choice we make every day, from the moment we arrive on this Earth to the moment we leave.

Soon, you'll make this choice, as well. You'll look at your own parents and consider your own family, and decide how you will feel about us and your history, our ancestors, and their legacies.

Know our ghosts will follow you always, throughout your life as your shadow, making sure that even in your solitude you're never alone.

NOTE ON SOURCES

This book starts with a note to the reader—a declaration, really—that it's a work of nonfiction. It is the product of original reporting and extensive research as filtered through me—my brain, my perspective, and my experiences. I interviewed my family members and dozens of members of the Iranian student movement. I spoke with those who knew my parents and those who didn't. I spoke with those who were active in the anti-shah movement in the United States, Europe, and Iran.

I supplemented these accounts with archival research, record requests, and old news stories. Not just those I found in broadsheets like the *New York Times*, the *Washington Post*, and the *Chicago Tribune*, but also hundreds of reports filed by reporters at United Press International, the Associated Press, and long-defunct wire agencies. I poured over gossip and society columns from the 1950s, 1960s, and 1970s and lost many hours digging through news archives and databases, like the American Archive of Public Broadcasting and the Bay Area Television Archive—treasure troves both. Two articles by reporter Andrew Veitch, published in the *Sydney Morning Herald* on December 14, 1983, proved especially useful. They helped me get a sense of life inside Evin Prison during the weeks and months before my father's death. I was also able to get a copy of CBS's *Nightline* program that aired on December 24, 1983. My father's trial is available, in part and in whole, on YouTube.

I also traveled to each place I write about, with the exception of Iraq and Yemen, both countries that have been turned into war zones by foreign nations like the United States and Iran. I used newspapers, books, newsreels, and documentaries from and about the periods I write about, to get a sense of the people, fashions, and rhythms of every place I mention. Each event detailed in these pages, whether the takeover of the Iranian consulate in San Francisco, the 2500-year celebrations in Persepolis, or the People's Park Riots in Berkeley, was checked against eyewitness accounts or newsreels, reports, and stills.

I relied heavily on my own personal family archive, which was kept in my mother's filing cabinet and was filled with her documents and transcripts, records of her life, as well as my father's and grandmother's lives. My mother's account of her cancer was found in my stepfather's records and given to me by Leila Arsanjani.

I'm deeply indebted to the librarians at the archives of Stanford's Hoover Institution, the Lyndon B. Johnson Presidential Library, the Missouri University of Science and Technology, and Monterey High School. They went out of their way to help me, emailing me scanned documents, letting me linger in reading rooms, sharing papers I didn't know existed, and patiently answering all my questions. I also used resources of the Richard Nixon Foundation and the Ronald Reagan Presidential Library.

Courthouse records, online archives, and the Freedom of Information Act libraries of United States government agencies were exceedingly helpful. I used the National Security Archives and declassified records released by the Department of State, the Central Intelligence Agency, and the Federal Bureau of Investigation. The entire CIA records of Operation Ajax were published by the *New York Times* online. The Anglo-Iranian Oil Company case, which was brought to the International Criminal Court (*United Kingdom v. Iran*) in 1952, can also be accessed online.

An April 1967 issue of the brilliant *Ramparts* magazine investigates the connection between the CIA, American Friends of the Middle East, and the birth of the Iranian Student Association. The entire issue is a fascinating exploration of how the United States' intelligence agencies tried and failed to manipulate the international student movement during the Cold War.

I spent an untold number of hours reading articles, histories, biographies, and memoirs about the people and the period. Here are just a few titles:

The Life and Times of the Shah by Gholam Reza Afkhami

Women in Exile by Mahnaz Afkhami

The Shah by Abbas Milani

All the Shah's Men: An American Coup and Roots of Middle East Terror by Stephen Kinzer

Losing Hearts and Minds: American-Iranian Relations and International Education During the Cold War by Matthew K. Shannon

An Answer to History by Mohammad Reza Shah Pahlavi

Countercoup: The Struggle for Control of Iran by Kermit Roosevelt

America's Great Game: The CIA's Secret Arabists and the Shaping of the Modern Middle East by Hugh Wilford

The Limits of Whiteness: Iranian Americans and the Everyday Politics of Race by Neda Maghbouleh

West Germany and the Global Sixties: The Anti-Authoritarian Revolt, 1962–1978 by Timothy Scott Brown

The Imagination of the New Left: A Global Analysis of 1968 by George Katsiaficas

1969: The Year Everything Changed by Rob Kirkpatrick

Berkeley at War: The 1960s by W. J. Rorabaugh

When I began this project, scholarly articles and books on the Iranian student movement were hard to come by. Now, there are more resources available, and more research is being done by Iranian

Americans and people of Iranian descent. It's a rich and unique area of study, one I can't wait to watch develop.

There are four memoirs that have deeply influenced my work. The filmmaker and authors showed me how weird, malleable, and beautiful this form could be.

The Stories We Tell, a documentary by Sarah Polley

The Fact of a Body: A Murder and a Memoir by Alex Marzano-Lesnevich

The Return: Fathers, Sons, and the Land In Between by Hisham Matar

The Father of All Things: A Marine, His Son, and the Legacy of Vietnam by Tom Bissell

ACKNOWLEDGMENTS

Here's a note, a second epilogue really, about my mother, aunts, uncle, cousin, and brother who escaped with me: they went on to become a celebrated editor, a lauded scientist, a passionate nurse, a committed civil engineer and bar owner, a devoted social worker, and a successful entrepreneur. Each one is extraordinary—the adults clawed their way from having nothing to having more than enough. They all brandish degrees and doctorates, own homes and businesses, and they've raised families, blood and adopted. They're brilliant, hilarious, resilient, and fierce. They survived crippling loss with their humanity, kindness, and decency intact. They taught us children to chase down our ambitions, withstand devastation, and discover our passions. If I told them every single day how much I love and admire them, it still wouldn't be enough. This book wouldn't exist without their patience, selflessness, and storytelling.

Indeed, the gestation period and birth of *They Said They Wanted Revolution* was long and at times arduous. I didn't have a clue what I had embarked on, and wouldn't have completed it if it wasn't for a great many people—family, friends, and colleagues—who stood by me, celebrated my successes, and held me through the myriad heartbreaks. From DC to Dubai, Oakland to Tehran, Algiers to Brooklyn, and points in-between, you know who you are. I wouldn't be standing without you. I thank you from the bottom of my heart. You are, each of you, extraordinary.

Like a child, this book is the legacy of many: Khaleh, who challenged me and generously shared correspondence, taped interviews, and oral histories—records that gave me insight into the past in my mother's own voice. Ameh, who didn't just sit for countless interviews and hours and hours and hours of conversation but who also shared her journals, her pain, and her perspective. She always came to my side when I needed her. Amu, who always told me stories about my father. He made sure I got to know my father, even just a little bit. Thank you for driving me round and round Berkeley, for supporting me, fact-checking me, and helping this project come alive. Daii, who sat through one interview after another. Thank you for sharing a lifetime of documents, pictures, and family history. I can't wait to read your kaleidoscopic life story, written in your voice. Shahrazad, who never let me forget that this was a story about people who were tied together through love and history. Nema Semnani, who trusted me with his camcorder loaded with hours and hours of footage that captured our mother's final year. It was an extraordinary privilege to have glimpsed the sweetness and intimacy of their love. Reza A., Niloo Z., Maryam Q., and the rest of my sprawling family, thank you for your steadfast love and support. Parviz Showkat, Jaleh Behroozi, Joyce Assmusen, Parviz Shakiban, Nasrine Pirnazar, Behrooz Mazandarani, Mansour Assadi, and so many others, thank you for sharing some sliver of your life stories. Without them, I would never have been able to write about the Confederation, my parents, and all the rest.

To all the former members of the Confederation, to my family friends and distant relations, and to all the others who spoke to me on and off the record: I'm forever indebted to you for your time and your honesty. Thank you for picking up the phone when I called, for all the emails, documents, and YouTube clips that you sent my way. Thank you for the many coffees, lunches, and dinners. Thank you for inviting me into your homes and your offices. Thank you for sharing some of your past. Thank you for holding my hand and letting me hold yours. Thank you especially for your vulnerability and wisdom.

It's true that scratching out a first draft is often a solitary practice, but in order for it to come to life, it needs readers, editors, and critics. I was lucky enough to have so many people who helped this project along the way: Merete Mueller read seemingly infinite versions of this manuscript and always found something kind to say about each one. I don't know how she did it. Jana Pruden taught me embroidery and told me to write when I told her I couldn't anymore. She sent me emergency writing kits and set up our first Friendency. Adriane Quinlan became my writing partner as I made my way through the final iterations of this book. She helped make this whole mess fun again. Kristina Gaddy asked me hard questions I needed to answer. Stephanie Gorton Murphy was with me, from the first word to the last. I'm forever grateful. Emily Ethridge was the book's first editor. She's done all her good deeds forever. Parisa Saranj and Hadi Fallahpisheh translated all the Persian I threw at them. Nilo Tabrizy is a true friend and brilliant photographer. Mina Jafari made the cover come to life. Noreen Malone very generously helped me get to the nutgraf, while Vanessa Mobley set a high bar, one I can only hope I cleared.

Revolution began as my graduate thesis at Goucher College. It is, in many ways, a product of those years when I learned the art and business of writing nonfiction. I couldn't have done it without that community: Suzannah Lessard, who saw this project for what it could be and gave me the space to figure it out. Jacob Levenson, who urged me to be brave and do my job and do it well. Diana Hume George, who taught me to write deliberately and with purpose. The late Richard Todd, who somehow believed this story would exist. Ginny McReynolds, Memsy Price, Rachel Dickinson, Jean Guerrero, Nick Tabor, Adam Valen Levinson, Theo Emery, Leslie Rubinkowski, and all the rest: thank you all for believing in the story, the reporter, and the writer. Because of you I am changed.

I'm hugely grateful to the Jonathan Logan Family Foundation and the Logan Nonfiction Program for giving me the time and space to write. Thank you for introducing me to a community of writers, reporters, documentarians, and artists. It was an absolute privilege to learn from them all, but especially Katherine E. Standefer, who showed me what it means to lay oneself bare on the page; Hussein Kesvani, who taught me the power of pushing through self-doubt; and Linda Yablonsky, who taught me what it means to commit to this work with your whole self. I'm also indebted to the NYSCA/NYFA Artists Fellowship—the grant meant so much more than cash; it was a sign that I should keep going. Thank you to John Summers, the former editor of the Baffler, and Michelle Legro, former editor of Longreads, who published excerpts of this book's earlier drafts.

My chosen family always gave me a place to run to and to write in: Jan and Dick Shafer, Clare and Brian Buchner, Kathleen Shafer, James Deweese, David Storey, and Jill and Mike Deweese Frank. This book literally wouldn't exist without their support and generosity. I probably wouldn't either. Meredith Dean and Colby Itkowitz, Sarah Smaller-Swift, and Chelsea Heffernan, who love me so fiercely and so well. I'd walk through fire for you. Sean Cole, who listened to me grapple with this beast in all the dining rooms and along all the sidewalks in New York City.

My wonderful agent, Bridget McCarthy, has the patience of a saint. Thank you for your comments, your support, and your kindness. Thank you for always picking up the phone and for guiding me through the last part of this long journey. Here's to the next one. Emma Borges-Scott and Alia Hanna Habib, who helped me along my way.

To my team at Little A, especially Hafizah Geter, who bought the proposal; Shari McDonald Strong, who edited the manuscript; and Carmen Johnson, who shepherded it to life. I'm forever grateful to you for believing in this story and this writer. Your insights and guidance helped me find my way to the heart of the story.

And, finally, Daniel, when I'm with you, I am home. I love you.